THE RICHES WITHIN

Other Hay House Titles by Dr. John F. Demartini

***The Breakthrough Experience:** A Revolutionary New Approach to Personal Transformation*

***Count Your Blessings:** The Healing Power of Gratitude and Love*

***The Heart of Love:** How to Go Beyond Fantasy to Find True Relationship Fulfillment*

How to Make One Hell of a Profit and Still Get to Heaven

You Can Have an Amazing Life . . . in Just 60 Days!

THE RICHES WITHIN

Your Seven Secret Treasures

Dr. John F. Demartini

HAY HOUSE, INC.
Carlsbad, California • New York City
London • Sydney • Johannesburg
Vancouver • Hong Kong • New Delhi

Published and distributed in the United States by: Hay House, Inc.: www.hayhouse.com • ***Published and distributed in Australia by:*** Hay House Australia Pty. Ltd.: www.hayhouse.com.au • ***Published and distributed in the United Kingdom by:*** Hay House UK, Ltd.: www.hayhouse.co.uk • ***Published and distributed in the Republic of South Africa by:*** Hay House SA (Pty), Ltd.: www.hayhouse.co.za • ***Distributed in Canada by:*** Raincoast: www.raincoast.com • ***Published in India by:*** Hay House Publishers India: www.hayhouse.co.in

Editorial supervision: Jill Kramer • *Design:* Tricia Breidenthal

The people in the stories in this book are, in some cases, composites. In every case, names have been changed to protect the privacy of the individuals.

The author of this book does not dispense medical advice or prescribe the use of any technique as a form of treatment for physical, emotional, or medical problems without the advice of a physician, either directly or indirectly. The intent of the author is only to offer information of a general nature to help you in your quest for emotional and spiritual well-being. In the event you use any of the information in this book for yourself, which is your constitutional right, the author and the publisher assume no responsibility for your actions.

Library of Congress Cataloging-in-Publication Data

Demartini, John F.
The riches within : your seven secret treasures / John F. Demartini. -- 1st ed.
p. cm.
ISBN-13: 978-1-4019-1826-2 (tradepaper) 1. Self-actualization (Psychology) I. Title.
BF637.S4D45 2008
158.1--dc22

2007030790

ISBN: 978-1-4019-1826-2

11 10 09 08 5 4 3 2
1st edition, March 2008
2nd edition, June 2008

Printed in the United States of America

To those who intuitively sense they have within their innermost being a great, buried treasure. A treasure that, when it's discovered and harnessed, can unleash a power so vast that they will sit in awe and inspiration just contemplating their newly revealed and awakened potential. May The Riches Within: Your Seven Secret Treasures open your heart and inspire your mind to newer and ever-greater possibilities and achievements. May it help you recognize your magnificent brilliance.

CONTENTS

INTRODUCTION

"Go to your bosom; Knock there,
and ask your heart what it doth know."
— William Shakespeare

You possess seven secret treasures—incredible riches already within you. When you uncover them, they will shine so brightly that *who you are* will be emblazoned on the heart of the world and even beyond it.

That's a bold statement, isn't it? Yet I know it to be true.

After working with countless people both in seminar settings and one-on-one, I've discovered something amazing. Every single person was greater—meaning more richly endowed with both mortal and immortal attributes, personal treasures—than he or she was consciously aware of and therefore demonstrating at any given time. That's a fascinating aspect of human nature: Our greatness can stay buried under layers of illusion, like the underside of an iceberg, yet our souls constantly prompt us to dive down and discover it so that we can reveal our true brilliance.

Why else would you be prompted even to pick up a book like this, if some part of you wasn't urging you on, letting you know that there's more to you than you may be aware of right now? Somewhere inside, you know that by reading something like *The Riches Within,* you might discover more of your own magnificence.

If you do more than just read the words here—that is, if you follow through on the suggested actions, you'll have the opportunity to embrace new ideas, enhance your experience of life, and expand your mind. You'll begin excavating those buried treasures and . . .

- Learn how to maximize the potential of your body, health, and well-being
- Discover how to have more fulfilling relationships and more love in your life
- See the strength you already possess
- Develop as a natural leader
- Uncover ways to build your financial wealth, and realize that everybody—including you—deserves prosperity
- Awaken inspiration and experience awe at the wonders around you every day
- Reveal your professional power by doing what you love and loving what you do
- Awaken to your own immortality and live a life of greatness

I've done my best to communicate simply, although I've also strived not to oversimplify or slip into jargon. My aim is to make inspiring ideas and principles speak to *you,* whether this is the first book you've ever read about your own power or if you're a seasoned student of self-actualization. We'll cover a broad range of materials encompassing your whole life, and even extending beyond your mortal existence.

Why contemplate something more than your existence right now? Why consider immortality? Because, if you're like most people, you consciously or unconsciously yearn to create or craft some form of lasting influence or an *immortal* expression beyond today, beyond your mere physical existence. For instance, you may believe in and desire a spiritual afterlife. Or you'd love to leave your most creative ideas and inspiring thoughts to posterity, to build a service-providing company that lasts after you leave the helm, to have more money at the end of your life than life at the end of your money, to produce offspring who carry your name, to make your contributive mark in social history, or even to discover a "fountain of youth." Your immortal legacy yearns for expression. In any case, *The Riches Within* will assist you in mining your greatest hidden treasures and help you awaken your most empowered and authentic self.

As in my previous books, each chapter of this work offers you several easily actionable items—in fact, this book may be filled with more practical activities than anything I've ever presented before. In addition to these items presented within the main text, I've also included instructions for my premiere methodology, The Demartini Method®. It appears in Appendix A as a ready reference since so much of what you'll be reading and learning about here depends on balancing your mind's perceptions—integrating two seemingly opposite ideas to come to a completely new perspective that will expand you into an ever-greater sphere of thought, influence, and love.

The Only Things That Can Get in Your Way

Everyone experiences what at first appear to be obstacles in life. That's a given. What may not be so obvious is that the only things capable of truly stopping you are fear and guilt. Yet these two emotions can't hold you back if you deal with them directly. If you find yourself feeling worried and afraid, experiencing regret and remorse, being immobilized, or seeming to be thrown "off course," all you have to do is bring these illusory emotions into *balance,* which is something this book will help you do.

A long time ago, I was talking with a neighbor who was working in her yard as I was pulling weeds around my house. She was over 80 years of age at the time, and she said, "John, if you don't plant flowers, you're always going to be pulling weeds!" I thought about that, how putting in a few things that you love will squeeze out those things you'd prefer not to grow. So I planted some "flowers" (the only thing I had on hand were some beans), and to my surprise, they sprouted. And soon enough, there was no room for weeds! I've since learned that the mind is the same way: If you don't plant flowers in the garden of the mind, then you'll forever be pulling weeds.

That's how it is with the fear and guilt that keep your treasures "secret" and hidden from you, overgrown with weeds and buried deep. The way to deal with these weedy emotions is to put them into balanced perspective. The quality of your life is based upon the quality of the questions you ask, and quality questions are those that balance out your perceptions and resultant actions. For example, if you think you're going to "lose" something or someone, you're wise to ask yourself about the opposite possibilities: *What am I going to "gain"?* If you think you might "fail" at something, figure out how the opposite could be true, too: *Where is my "success"? What is the benefit of the so-called failure?*

These kinds of balancing questions form the foundation of the essential methods presented in this book. Throughout, you'll read about various ways of balancing all kinds of myths and misperceptions about yourself, others, and the world in which you live. That's because one of the greatest impediments to personal evolution is an exaggerated, lopsided expectation—one that reflects neither the magnificent order of the universe nor the brilliance of every individual in it. Quite often, people expect themselves to be something they're not. Can you see how self-depreciating that could be? (That's not a typo: I really mean self-depreciating, or devaluing.) Can you see how demoralizing and diminishing such delusions or fantasies might be?

There's a difference between fantasy and big vision, of course. Big visions are those dreams that are doable and aligned with your values. Fantasies are not achievable and don't align with your values, so you won't act on them and you won't keep working toward them even if you get yourself started—and then you'd beat yourself up for "falling short." Whatever truly aligns with your heart, whatever you feel certain about, whatever you know you were put on the planet to live by and for, constitute your inspirations. They're some of your most radiant riches. You can't help but follow them once you've opened the treasure chest and looked inside.

The Seven Fears—Don't Let Them Get in Your Way!

I'll say it again: Deep within you, you already know how brilliant you are. And the reason why you might not fully realize it right now is because there's some fear tarnishing your shine. Perhaps you've heard before that there are seven primary fears in life, a perfect complement to our seven secret treasures. Nelson Mandela said, in his rendition of statements in *A Course in Miracles,* that we're frightened of our power. We're not frightened of our smallness; we're frightened of our magnificence. So true! We sometimes let these seven fears stop us from going after our dreams and visions.

When you bump up against them, use this book to help you neutralize their hold on you, to set you free to pursue your own magnificence, which is the greatest treasure you possess.

First Fear: Intellectual Shortcomings

One fear that prevents people from revealing who they really are, from uncovering all their treasures, is an underlying anxiety that they're just not smart enough. They believe they don't have the academic degree or the knowledge or the mental or memory capacity to accomplish their dreams.

In the very first chapter of this book, you'll discover that this doesn't have to stop you. Every one of us has been endowed with genius—even those of us who are told we *aren't* smart and we "can't" develop a formidable intellect. I should know; when I was a boy, a teacher informed my parents that I was learning disabled and would never amount to much. But this type of pronouncement means nothing in the face of your genius! Keep reading, and you'll learn how I overcame this false prophecy—and how to unlock your own genius.

Second Fear: Physical Inadequacies

Maybe you think that you don't have the right body—you're not tall enough, you're not good-looking enough, you're too old, or you don't have the right profile or the right energy. Sometimes, people's perceptions about their bodies can stop them from creating an amazing life for themselves. Sometimes, they don't feel they could sustain the effort it would take either to get there or to keep it once it's achieved. Let me encourage you: Doing what you love and loving what you do makes you feel younger and more vital! I'll even go so far as to say that it improves your looks and extends your life.

I guarantee that if you do what you love, and appreciate what your financial resources can offer the world, you're likely to make more money than you would otherwise, and it's been shown that people who have greater financial wealth in their lives will live longer. Your physical body will adapt to those things that you're clear about in your heart. Remember, there's always somebody who beats the odds. There's the man who's short who ends up playing basketball and the lady who's an "ugly duckling" who becomes a supermodel. They had a dream, and they let nothing about their physical selves stop them.

Your body serves in so many ways. Learn more about how to unlock the secrets of immortality in the chapter on your physical treasures.

Third Fear: Failure

The fear of failure can break you down and keep you from believing in your own capacity. What most people do when they're confronted with this fear is focus on something they know they can do, and they don't challenge themselves. Ultimately, they deny themselves the opportunity to do what they'd most love because of this fear . . . but if you live your life without doing what you love, would that be any less of a so-called failure? The truth is that if you're really committed to something and go for it but you "fail," you'll get right back up and start again—that's what I'd rather do!

As you read this book, you'll no doubt start to redefine your idea of failure—not seeing it as a tragic ending, but instead as a feedback system to balance your perception about how it impacts your life. There are always gifts in great "failures," just as there are always drawbacks in great "successes." You'll find some of your greatest treasures tucked under the weight of a perceived failure. Take a look and you'll discover something magnificent under each one.

Fourth Fear: Scarcity

An excuse I hear all the time from people who know what they'd love to do in their lives but just can't bring themselves to do it, is that if they pursue the dream, they might lose money, or they might not make enough money. In my experience, doing what you love and loving what you do are the most powerful ways to build wealth. I believe that you can't really fail unless you're working against yourself. If you're clear about your values, your dreams, and your objectives of true service in life, *you will achieve.* That includes achievements with money, too, as you'll learn in the chapter on your financial treasures. What's more, if you're willing to say you don't know everything and get some help, that will expedite your accomplishments and bring you the rewards you deserve for pursuing the dream you love.

Fifth Fear: Society's Judgments

Another fear that stops people is the fear of being rejected by the world around them. If they pursue their dreams, they worry, ridicule and rejection will follow them wherever they go. I once consulted with a gentleman who was a lawyer, and he'd done everything his parents wanted. He'd gone all the way through law school, gotten into a practice—and then hit a plateau. He'd never really thrived as an attorney. When he came to my program called The Breakthrough Experience®, where I help people break through their perceived obstacles and get clear about their lives, he started crying. This was a man who was trained to keep a poker face, but he was confronting the truth of his own soul, and it made him weep.

The truth was that he loved cars, especially acquiring and selling them, "wheeling and dealing," as he called it. So I asked him, "Why haven't you made your living from this?"

He said, with tears in his eyes, "I just never thought that I could be respected in that kind of profession."

Using the tools you'll be reading about in this book, this man came to see that most of his fears were just projections, and that for every person who would reprimand him for his choices, there would be someone else who would praise him. Today, this former attorney makes an incredible living selling classic cars—he loves what he does, so people love to deal with him. His heart is in it, and his energy and vitality bring him great fulfillment. Read the chapter on vocational treasures to find out exactly how he made this powerful change in his life.

Sixth Fear: Rejection

The next fear that can stop you from going after your dreams is the fear of losing loved ones. Maybe there are parents who say, "You can't make money at that." Or maybe you have children and you think you can't afford to take the risk; it's too chancy for you. Or your spouse may leave you if you go after your dreams! The people around you may think you're crazy.

But you know what? Going through life without doing what you love and loving what you do *is* crazy! It's wise to take the risk. And when you take a wisely calculated risk, you give other people permission to live without fear. You give them permission to be true to themselves, too. This kind of relationship, one where people care about one another—not just because they're related but because they honor one another's differences and are truly grateful for them—actually has a kind of magnetism that can help you in your endeavors. Read more about this in the chapter on unity and family treasures.

Seventh Fear: Authority

Many people are afraid of not living up to the belief system of some "authority." Quite often, this authority takes the form of a religious institution, although it can be any body from which you fear judgment and punishment: academic authority, parental authority, professional authority, and so on. In other words, you might be afraid you're not going to live up to their morals and ethics and other rules, so you stop yourself from pursuing what you really love because you're afraid that somebody may think it's "wrong."

The Oracle of Delphi counseled, "Know thyself, be thyself, and love thyself." I wonder what would happen if all of us were true to ourselves? Throughout this book, and especially in the chapter on leadership and your social treasures, you'll be reexamining the validity of authority figures you've chosen, and stepping up to become your own highest authority. Imagine what you can do and be when you put all of your treasures to wise use and wield them with love!

Remove Fears with Balance

Let's define *fear* as an assumption that you're going to experience, through your senses or your imagination, *more loss than gain, more negative than positive, more pain than pleasure,* from somebody or yourself. Whenever you have fear, you presume that you can have one side without the other. In this way, fear is always an illusion: The truth is that life always, in every case, gives you both sides.

Every event of your life is like a magnet with both a positive and a negative polarity, always a pair of opposites. Therefore, if you think there's a loss, it's wise to look for the gain. If you perceive a negative, you're wise to look for the positive. If you think there's a challenge, look for the support—and vice versa, all down the line. Whenever you're in a state of fear, such as the fear of not appeasing some authority, or of not knowing enough, ask the opposite question!

For example: "If I think I don't know enough, where *do* I know enough? How is it, with my knowledge, that I can accomplish what I would love even more powerfully and effectively than if I had some other form of knowledge?" Neutralize your fears by asking the exact opposite question! If I fear I'm going to be rejected by somebody, I ask, "What would be the benefit if I were rejected?" And at the same time, "Who would be supporting me at that moment?"

When you ask a question that neutralizes that imbalanced perspective, you bring it back into balance, and the fear dissolves as if by magic! If you feel that somehow you're going to fail, ask yourself, *If I do "fail," how could that benefit me? How could I use that to my advantage? If I seem to be "failing" on this pathway, where am I "succeeding" in another way?*

Think about the usual struggle parents face, particularly mothers, who more frequently face the dilemma of child care versus work. If she's a professional woman, she may feel the "loss" of her worth in her career if she stops working to take care of the baby herself. If she puts the child in the care of someone else, she may feel as if she's "failing" as a mother. But what happens if she makes her choice and then asks herself these questions to balance her perspective? If she sincerely pursues the answers—her own unique set of answers to the questions—then this very "problem" may actually cause her to awaken to each and every one of her seven secret treasures!

Could such a woman come to realize that pursuing her profession benefits her entire family by not only providing income but also by setting an example of doing what you love? What might a child learn from that? Or could such a woman come to realize that her real calling in life is directly nurturing her child, no matter what ideas she may have held previously about her worth being tied to the workplace? Or . . . or . . . or . . . ? The treasures such a woman might find in searching her mind and heart about such questions could be of inestimable value.

Confronting, questioning, and resolving your fears and "failures"—and being genuinely interested in an honest shift to a new perspective—demands that you be open to see and manage paradoxes, or seeming opposites. And it also demands that you be prepared for those opposites to be present everywhere, all the time.

Along your journey of living a magnificent life and awakening the secret treasures that you have within you, you're going to be supported *and* you're going to be challenged. Your tendency is to want to be supported more than challenged. The reality is that life always gives you both, because you need both to develop as a human being. This is living fully. This is the march of the soul. This is the human experience.

Let neither the pleasures nor the pains, neither the support nor the challenge, neither buildups nor put-downs keep you from your dreams! Just see that both sides are feedback mechanisms to help you along your journey. Without the presence of both positive and negative, you'd be addicted to one and avoid the other. Realize that you can live up to your magnificence only if you embrace both!

Questioning teaches you to look, and suddenly brings you to timelessness and love. If you don't take the time to look, you simply react; and everything you continue to perceive as one-sided adds another layer of debris, dampening your brilliance, further burying your seven secret treasures. When you perceive events as equilibrated and freed and taken from material emotions, you're liberated as you transform the misperceptions into energy and light, which enlighten your mind and heart! When you see both sides at the same moment, you have an enlightened mind with synchronous thought. In that moment, you suddenly realize that you're not reprimanded and you're not praised. You are simply loved.

Love is the synthesis of attraction and repulsion, praise and reprimand, nice and mean, kind and cruel. When we get infatuated, we can't see the downsides. When we get resentful, we can't see the upsides. In actuality, both are occurring at the same time. If we suddenly see both of them synchronously, we enter into the world Thomas Aquinas called *synchronicity.* If we see one without the other, we live in a world that's called *diachronicity.* Diachronicity means living through time; and *synchronicity* is living in a *timeless mind, ageless body,* as Deepak Chopra likes to call it.

I'll say it again: Our addiction in our society, the opiate of the masses, the junk under which most of our treasures are hidden, is the idea that we're supposed to have one side without the other. We're supposed to be kind but never cruel, sweet but never bitter, and positive but never negative. Life isn't that way, but we have this fantasy that it's going to be! Someday we'll get there . . . when we are perfect, we'll be happy . . . and it is never happening! Many people pin all their hopes on an afterlife where one side rules, and all those things we're infatuated with in the present magnify into some palace in the sky. Such people completely miss out on the balanced magnificence of what is already here, right now!

Take a moment to reflect on the amazing order you can awaken to in your life right now: At the moment of praise and reprimand, right here, the praise that supports is balanced by the reprimand that challenges. One makes you dependent and the other keeps you independent. You need both in order to grow and maximize your development!

One day when I was at the British Open in Scotland, I was walking alongside legendary golfer Tiger Woods. He had someone who appeared to be a psychologist there with him to give him feedback. If he were to make a magnificent shot, and perhaps feel a little elated and excited, the fellow would say, "Yes, but we still have this many holes to finish." He calms him down so that Tiger doesn't get too elated. If his shot goes into the sand trap, the same guiding assistant says, "You're very close. That means that you take on the pressure, which is when you do your best!" He gives him feedback to balance him and hone him in on his balanced, authentic, and most powerful self so that he doesn't get too up and elated or too down and depressed.

If you'd love to unveil your seven secret treasures, start with Tiger's wisdom of his sport: *Take no credit; take no blame! Just keep focused on the game! Focus on the mission and chief aim!* Start and live your day by embracing both sides of life. That is fulfillment, instead of half-fillment! Imagine life as a magnet and embrace both sides of your daily magnet in the dreams and the opportunities of your life. It lures the treasure out of its "hiding" place. It's the magnetism of opportunity!

This entire book is designed to help you recognize this magnificence and magnetism in you, just as you are. You don't need to "fix" anything in yourself, yet I'd love to offer you many different ways to polish all the riches you've been given. Realize that your seven secret treasures don't have to remain hidden any longer. Turn the page and you open the treasure chest just a crack, and no doubt you'll immediately see the glimmer of what's inside . . . *you!*

CHAPTER ONE

Genius: Your Mental Treasures

"A good mind possesses a kingdom."
— Seneca the Younger

"Who are you?" I asked.

We were in a hotel conference room, and I was leading one of my seminars for about 100 people. The man who'd just stood up and said his name for everyone looked perplexed. Then he spoke slowly and with more volume: "My. Name. Is. *Joe.*"

Chuckling, I said, "Joe, I'm asking who you are, not your name."

He laughed, too, and then said, "Sorry, I thought you were hard of hearing. Anyway, I'm a high school biology teacher from Philadelphia." And a second or two later, he added, "A divorced dad who loves his kids."

"Okay, thanks. But I'm asking you a more abstract question: Who are you, really?"

Joe blinked and then responded: "I'm a human body . . . animated by a complex nervous system." He seemed pleased with himself for coming up with that one.

We went on like this, until we finally arrived at the essence of the question and everyone in the room got it: **Each of us has an incredible, immortal mind—consciousness, an intelligent and creative force. That's who we really are.** I explained to the group that we were talking about more than a brain, of course. You're not just your gray matter any more than you're an arm or a gallbladder. You're not merely a job, a relationship, an achievement, or any of those things with which people often over-identify.

Instead, you're the culmination of those intangible, ineffable treasures of the soul, which we can also call the riches of the mind: your *intention* and *inspiration,* your *receptiveness* and *perceptiveness,* your *intellect* and *reason.*

Each of these gems can be brought to a high shine, no matter how old or young you may be. As a boy, I was labeled "learning disabled" and was told that I wouldn't amount to much, but even someone like me always possessed *every one* of these priceless gifts and was capable of making the most of them. For some people, these treasures get buried for a while, but they do exist in equal measure inside all of us. (Yes, I said "equal measure." That is, both you and Einstein were given the same raw material. More on that later.) Some people tuck their gifts away and forget where they put them. No matter how buried, tarnished, or neglected yours may be, this chapter will help you rediscover all the treasures of your amazing mind.

Your Mental Treasure #1: Questions

When I was 17, I met Paul C. Bragg, who became one of the greatest teachers in my life. This lively white-haired man presented an inspiring health- and human-potential lecture one evening, which first opened my eyes to the principles and laws of the universe. When he was done, he looked at all of us in the audience and said, "You have ten minutes. Think about what you'd love to dedicate your life to. Tonight, you're going to determine your destiny."

Something changed for me that night as I sat on the floor and reviewed my life up to that point. At the time, I was a surf bum, living on the beach in a tent with some buddies. I'd dropped out of high school at 14, hit the road on my own, and wound up in Hawaii. I was also still weak from having just survived strychnine poisoning from an island plant I'd been eating for breakfast nearly every day.

In my mind's eye, I saw Mrs. McLaughlin, my first-grade teacher, announcing to my parents: "I'm afraid your son will never read, write, communicate, or amount to anything much. He won't go very far in life. He's got learning disabilities."

Then I saw myself hitchhiking through El Paso, Texas, and I remembered the wise homeless man I'd met who had told me, "There are only two things they can never take away from you: your love and your wisdom!"

I also saw myself lying in my tent, almost dead.

And then I opened my eyes and looked up to see Paul Bragg sitting there, alive, vibrant, and inspired—dedicated to something, urging me on to my purpose!

Suddenly I thought to myself, *I know what I'd love to do!* I knew I'd love to dedicate myself to what this man had talked about: these universal laws, particularly as they related to the body, mind, and spirit—to health. I thought, *I want to become a master teacher, healer, and philosopher like this man! And I want to travel the world, set foot in every country on the face of the earth, and share my research findings!*

Next, Paul Bragg directed us through a guided-imagery meditation where I entered into a state of inspiration and suddenly saw myself standing on a balcony over a giant square, speaking to hundreds of thousands of people.

That was the last thing I would have imagined showing up in my mind as I sat there in the little Sunset Recreation Room on the North Shore of Oahu, but that was what I saw. My vision was so vivid and clear that I felt as if I were living it already. That picture has stayed with me ever since—a revelation so inspiring that it still brings tears to my eyes.

When I left that evening, I set out on a mission to understand the power of the human mind and body at the deepest level, and that quest has led me to study more than 260 disciplines and read more than 28,500 texts. All because one very healthy old man asked me a riveting question: **"What is your destiny?"**

He was also the first person to suggest to me that I was a genius. You can imagine how unbelievable I found that at the time. But he insisted that we're all geniuses, and he gave me an assignment on the spot: Every day I was to say to myself: *I am a genius, and I apply my wisdom.* Even though I didn't feel like a genius, and even though I had no evidence that I was a genius or possessed any recognizable wisdom, I was supposed to just keep saying these words of power to myself every day. (You'll find these and even more words of power for *you* to use at the end of each chapter in this book.)

Soon thereafter, I found myself being inspired in an afternoon meditation to return to Texas and visit my parents. Not long after I arrived, my mom and dad both encouraged me to take a GED, or high school equivalency exam, and then a college entrance exam—both of which I passed, thereby surprising everyone, including myself. I then attempted to do equally as well in my first college class (history), but I failed my first test and felt devastated by my grade. My mother found me distraught on the living-room floor, crying because of it. She shared with me some of the most powerful words of my life: "No matter what you end up doing, son, your father and I are going to love you, no matter what." That deeply touched and inspired me to make a promise to myself that *I would master reading, studying, teaching, healing, and philosophy; and I would do whatever it took, travel whatever distance, and pay whatever price to offer my services of love!*

Imagine how startled and grateful I was a couple of years later when I was sitting in a library studying for a calculus test, and a number of students asked me to tutor them—and I overheard one of them whispering, "That Demartini, he's a frigging genius." There was some evidence out there after all!

None of my other surfing buddies who'd lived in the tent with me had gone to hear Paul Bragg speak that day. What happened to them? One died of a cocaine addiction. One is in a nursing home because he overdosed on drugs and now has persistent psychiatric issues. The other is homeless. That was my destiny, too, before Paul Bragg asked me to choose my own future—before he asked me to use my mind and answer his powerful, empowering question.

The truth is, no matter what you ask yourself, your mind will come up with an answer. If you can conceive of a question, you can create an answer. Ask, *Where's the best beach to surf and do drugs?* Your mind will come up with something. Ask, *What kind of life would I love to lead?* It will come up with an answer, something that's uniquely your own as long as you persist and look into the depths of your heart, mind, and soul.

You are a genius. Can you see how potent these words of power are? Even if you're not already feeling like a genius, even if you don't think you have any evidence of being a genius yet, are you at least getting an inkling of the great cache of mental riches at your command?

Still don't believe me? Take some time now to ask yourself these questions:

- *Where is my mind already alert?*
- *Where is it creative?*
- *Where is it spontaneous?*
- *Where does it have the power to answer questions quickly?*

Don't cop out by saying, "It's not." *It is.* Ask yourself these questions until your amazing mind delivers an answer to you. Dig deep. And when you get an answer, write it down and acknowledge the treasure you've just uncovered.

Your Mental Treasure #2: Knowledge and Experience

How much time do you already spend reading, listening, or watching something that enriches you and expands your mind? It's a remarkable thing, really, that all it takes is *exposure* to great human creations for some of their greatness to rub off. As the saying goes, you can't put your hand into a pot of glue without some of it sticking.

You're wise to be discerning as you choose written material for reading; audio programs and music for listening; and TV programs, movies, and theater productions for watching. Look for those things with genius in them if you'd love to inspire the genius in you.

Fill your mind with great ideas—other people's great ideas. Below you'll find just some of the endless sources of knowledge and experience available to you.

Don't read good books.
Read the great ones.

The *Great Books of the Western World* series can be found in pretty much any library. These volumes contain classic writings from Aeschylus to Virgil and from ancient Greek and Roman philosophy and plays to contemporary science and literature. Talk about a treasure trove! **Dive into these books and you'll be immersed in genius.** And if you don't want to tackle the whole series, then be sure to read *The Syntopicon: An Index to the Great Ideas,* both volumes. Then read the biographies of the immortal geniuses in the beginning of each of the many volumes that follow. Look for the common threads of their lives and discover yourself in their childhoods or developing years. By doing this, you'll be reawakening your inner calling to express something magnificent. Each of us is an immortal in the making.

Beyond this series, hundreds of other great masters have left their writings and biographies for you to absorb. Reading about their thoughts, inventions, creations, or simply their lifestyles will make a difference in your outlook on life, stimulating greater and more magnificent ideas in your own mind. What a gift it is to receive one simple idea that can transform your life forever! Be sure to write down any ideas that sing true to your heart, whether they come directly from the masters' works or are stimulated by them. Start a computerized notebook or journal where you can keep a record of your inspirations.

Let your soul guide you to pursue specialized study, too. Do you realize that if you read 30 minutes each day in any field, you can be on the cutting edge of that field in just seven years? Devote an hour and you're there in four years. And if you read three hours a day, you could literally be on the cutting edge of a field in a year and a half or less!

Make your heart sing.

Everyone can hear special pieces of music that evoke tears of inspiration and feelings of gratitude and love, and some that compel creating or acting in ways that elevate the mind, body, and spirit. By listening to the great orchestra, opera, and symphony performances, you can fine-tune your appreciation of true harmony and beauty. The mathematics of sound and the inspired expressions of voice heighten your awareness of your own soul's callings. Harmonic vibrations can generate a desire for greater expression in your own being.

Surround yourself with grand music, with the classics that have stood the test of time. Listen to recordings, but also be sure to go to live performances, where you can feel the instruments hum in your nervous system, the percussion pulse in your veins. Fill your mind with the powerful vibrations of music that soar to the heavens and bring you back to Earth feeling more encouraged and alive than before.

Check out some naked ladies.

To awaken your genius and its appreciation for aesthetic beauty, either purchase or borrow some of the many quality books that contain full-color plates of the great paintings, sculptures, and other forms of art—or go see them in person at a museum. It's nearly impossible to walk through the Louvre in Paris or the Metropolitan in New York City without being deeply moved by what you see there and without feeling the pull to express your own inner genius. **Expose yourself to the great art and treasures of the world.**

See and be seen in the best places.

Start by going to a travel agency and asking for every brochure on every destination. Take them home and sift through the stack, cutting out pictures of every place you feel inspired to visit someday, or those that evoke some kind of longing or connection in you.

Be sure to consider locations that feature the great art and architecture of the world, including cathedrals, temples, monuments, statues, palaces, and any other masterpieces. Take a look at the great wonders of the world: the Pyramids of Giza, Stonehenge, the Colosseum in Rome, the Great Wall of China, the Leaning Tower of Pisa, Mount Everest, the Grand Canyon, the Northern

Lights, the Great Barrier Reef, the Galápagos Islands, the Panama Canal, the Golden Gate Bridge, Mount Fuji, Niagara Falls . . . you get the picture. Or you will, once you visit your travel agent.

Make this into a collage or simply keep the pictures handy so you can look at them at least once a week. **Start taking the first action steps to get you to the places that most call out to you, and be open to unexpected travel opportunities.** Organize your time so that you can visit at least some of the most awe-inspiring places in your lifetime. Realize that inspiration breeds creativity and awakens genius.

Stare into space.

In ancient times, people looked to the heavens for answers about life here on Earth. They viewed the heavenly bodies as the source of all life. These concentric spheres of space, with their wandering and fixed planets and stars, were a source of wonder. Their vastness gave direction and motivation to those who could see beyond the confines of terrestrial life. Their abstract nature stretched those who contemplated their spiritual harmonies to greater visions and callings.

Today, just as in times long past, you have a capacity for exploration and wonder. To gaze out at the far reaches of the cosmos gives you a sense of limitlessness and provides you with the open dimensions of space and time to contemplate unbounded planes of thought. Genius streams from such an astronomical stretch.

Go to your local planetarium and learn about the stars. Imagine yourself a star in the making.

Make it a goal to visit at least one great observatory. Arrange to view the heavens with the aid of some of the most powerful telescopes on Earth. Pick a star to focus on, make a wish, and then ask the star for a message. Wait for the message, and record it when it comes. A state of gratitude will hasten the message; often the vastness of the heavenly view alone will bring about an inspiration.

Follow your animal instincts.

What a gift it is to be able to experience the natural world of animals without even leaving your city, simply by visiting your local zoo. To see the array of colors, sounds, sizes, and shapes of all the incredible creatures ennobles your human experience. As you watch them, realize that these are the beings who have stood the test of time. Think about how they've directed human invention, including the airplane, the crane, and many others.

And if you can see animals living in nature, so much the better. If you don't feel the call to take an African safari, then visit a zoo that prides itself on natural habitats, such as the world-famous one in San Diego. And its sister wildlife preserve, the Wild Animal Park, is just a 45-minute drive to the north. It sits on 1,800 acres, allowing visitors to view exotic animals as they might be seen in their native lands. Your observations are much more valuable when you can see zebras loping in a herd or elephants patrolling the wide-open spaces. You get to see more of their natural beauty and behavior this way.

Without these creatures, humans wouldn't be where they are today. From designs to insights and from functions to curves, the great animals of the world have been an unequaled inspiration. Be grateful for them.

Stop and smell the roses.

You probably get up some mornings, walk outside, and totally miss the most magnificent creations available to your senses. Most of us do. But you can choose to appreciate what's literally right before your nose. From the beautiful, fragrant flowers that grow in almost every neighborhood to the incredible trees that teach us so much about the phases of earthly living, plants literally give us the breath of life. From the beginning, plants and people have mutually coexisted. Beyond the nutritional, medicinal, and oxygenating value of plants and trees, they also reflect a design of such beauty and order that when you deeply investigate their forms, your mind can only marvel.

Most people have lain under a large tree and stared up and out at the sun, observing the hundreds of tiny points of sunlight sparkling through the tree's leaves. Usually, a fresh idea arises from this most relaxing state, and some people have even noted the ratios of branches and leaves and discovered their musical harmonies or proportions. Even a breeze through a field of wheat can carry a message for those who pause to notice.

Take a walk in a park, field, or forest. Stop and listen wherever the whispering wind guides you to stand. Ask for nature's message in the moment, and listen with your heart.

Your Mental Treasure #3: Reflection

Whatever you see in other individuals, you have inside yourself. Not just some things, but all things, including what you most admire and what you most despise. In fact, the traits you persist in thinking are "too good" or "too bad" for you are the ones you simply haven't learned to fully embrace in yourself—but they're there, I assure you. I call this "the reflection principle": If you can recognize it in someone else, it's inside of you.

My book *The Breakthrough Experience* is all about this phenomenon, and it teaches you how to use The Demartini Method to realize that you have inside of you everything you see around you. If you think Einstein was a genius, know that you have genius in you, too. You may not have the same *form* of genius as he did, but your genius is there, nonetheless, in equal measure. The moment you realize that you have every trait you admire, and start recognizing the form it's in, it begins to surface. Out comes the buried treasure.

One client of mine dreamed of becoming a consultant to the leading Fortune 500 companies in the world, yet he was intimidated by their powerful leaders—the CEOs of those organizations. Because of this fear, my client was holding himself back from accomplishing his goal of being a great consultant to them. So I asked him to identify everything about these CEOs he admired and everything that intimidated him. When he had written those characteristics down, I told him to ask himself, *Where do I have that trait in some form?*

Initially, he dismissed this idea. "I don't have all of those! Maybe some, but not all."

"Look again," I told him.

"But I don't!" he insisted.

I encouraged, "Look again! Don't stop looking! Because the truth is *if you can spot it, you've got it!* It's like some buried treasure, and we just need to dig around until we find it."

Ultimately, he took on the challenge of finding every single trait he admired in those CEOs within himself. He identified where he had the power, the influence, the leadership, the skills, and the knowledge. It took him a while to actually awaken his appreciation of all that within himself, but to his credit, he did it. In just a day or two, he started to see a shift, and in about a week, he was seeing more deeply where he had every trait he admired in these enormously wealthy, successful CEOs. Within three months, he was completely clear that he was just as powerful, influential, skillful, knowledgeable, and every bit as much of a leader as the people he would love to have as his clients. In fact, during this period, one of the very people he had thought about in this exercise signed a contract with him.

So here's my challenge for you: Ask yourself, *Who is one of the most ingenious people I know? What are his or her traits? Where do I have those same traits?* Don't lie to yourself—don't say that you don't know or can't find it. Just dig!

Sometimes we think that other people have a better deal than us, but the reality is that we have the potential for just as great a deal as anyone else! Discover what mental power is inside of you!

Regularly, I do this exercise myself, searching for each trait of all the various Nobel Prize winners. Whether or not you have the goal of being a prize winner, can you see how empowering it would be to recognize yourself in such an esteemed crowd? One by one, I've read something about or by each Nobel laureate, especially biographies (which are readily available online). And as I do this, I note every single area of their lives that is similar to mine.

Earlier in my life, by identifying those ingenious traits within myself, not only did my confidence rise, but also the speed of my mind-powers grew and I started to recognize that I truly did have what they had. It wasn't missing for me—and it's not missing for you. It's simply in a valuable form you may never have recognized.

And so this has become a lifelong pursuit for me: Anytime I run across people I think possess great minds, I read their biographies and identify where we're similar. It's amazing what this has done for me—a man who couldn't read or write as a boy now sees himself in the company of recognized geniuses.

You know, the world treats you the way you treat yourself. If you value yourself, the world values you. Until you value yourself, no one else will. Likewise, if you don't give yourself permission to do something great, why would the world assist you? You must allow yourself to be great and do something extraordinary.

Your Mental Treasure #4: Attention

If you've read my other books, you're familiar with my discussion of values: Everyone has them, everyone has different ones, and the content and order of these values determines, almost entirely, your behavior. Whatever is highest on your value list is where your mind is sharp and alert, disciplined and focused. Whatever is lower on your value list is where you hesitate and procrastinate.

If you'd love to awaken your genius and fully tap the power of your mind, then you need to realize it will be in the area that's highest in your values.

I like to think of it this way: We all have areas of "attention surplus order" and areas of "attention deficit disorder." Consider a child, for instance, who's labeled with ADD. In truth, the same child may be able to sit for six or seven hours playing a video game, totally focused with an autographic and photographic mind for that game. Does the child really "have" ADD, then, if he or she can pay attention to something for so long? What it really means is that the child values the video games more than academics. That's just what's true for the child, and the label of ADD, in this light, is clearly a misnomer. Video games are this child's genius.

There's probably something like this going on for you. Unrecognized treasures remain buried inside you: treasures according to *your* values! Even if someone else labeled you with ADD, or if others haven't recognized your knowledge, your genius, or the power of your mind, just know that their estimation of your wisdom isn't really true for you.

In a later chapter, you'll be clarifying your values so you can see exactly where your genius resides. Maybe you already know where it is. Perhaps you're already aware of your highest value, which is where your mind is sharp and alert! And if you haven't discovered that yet, then for now know that deep in the earth where great diamonds are born, there's a geothermal power and pressure—and you have that same power and pressure inside you, ready to burst forth and explode with possibility.

Your Mental Treasure #5: Intention/Visualization

Imagine yourself living as you'd love your life to be. As you visualize this, you might start with some haziness and it may be a bit awkward, but take a moment to let the fog lift and the picture sharpen.

Intention and visualization were both significant parts of the movie *The Secret,* in which I was delighted to participate. That film has resulted in the mainstream media discussing the Law of Attraction, something I've been interested in and investigating ever since I sat in Paul Bragg's class all those years ago. So the truth is that the Law of Attraction isn't really a secret. Power athletes, most notably Tiger Woods, have talked often and openly about how they use visualization to bring results that they'd most deeply love to experience out of the realm of mind and into the tangible world.

I'm fond of saying that your vitality is directly proportional to the vividness of your vision. Your mind has the capacity to picture things in such detail that it literally impacts the quantum fields that surround you and permeate the universe.

Don't misunderstand me here, as some have misunderstood *The Secret.* I'm not saying that you should sit on a beanbag chair in your den and dream about millions of dollars falling down your chimney and into your lap—and expect that to be the trick. This isn't a magic show. This is about aligning your intention with *action:* using the power of your mind to shape and consciously create your reality.

After I heard Paul Bragg speak—after he spurred me to imagine my destiny—I didn't just go back to my tent and sit cross-legged in the sand to visualize. No, I got busy instead. I started taking steps immediately in pursuit of my new mission. I held fast to that vision—and now what I imagined at age 17 has become a reality for me. I'm living the exact life I saw for myself.

I know you're capable of doing the same, but maybe you've been afraid to go for it and allow that vision to come out. You may have let fear stop you in the past. You may have bought into the idea that you couldn't do it. You may have thought that you didn't have enough smarts to do it, or you may have thought that you'd fail if you went after what you really loved. You may have been afraid that you'd lose loved ones or that you'd be rejected.

But if you have a vision, you have the capacity to fulfill it. You may need assistance, you may seek guidance from others, and you may delegate things along the way, but the reality is that you can create your vision.

Start today. Visualize what you'd love in your life. If you can, cut out pictures and images of everything you'd love to create in your life. Create a storybook and a picture board of how you'd love to live. I still carry such a book with me everywhere I go—it depicts each one of the inspiring visions and dreams I have and serves as a reminder of what I'd love to do and become.

So I'm asking you to visualize your life the way you'd love it. Close your eyes and picture it, and become present with the ever-finer details. The power of intention will make things happen! Admire the treasure you have inside you to make your dreams come true. It works if you'll work it. So apply it!

Once the vision is clear, write it down and begin to affirm it as true today—not "I want to be a genius," but instead "I am a genius, and I apply my wisdom." Know that your innermost dominant thought becomes your outermost reality. Visualize, affirm, and think of exactly how you'd love your life to be.

As I mentioned earlier, to help you with this, at the end of each chapter in this book you'll find some "words of power." **Choose at least one or two of these and read them out loud seven times every day.** You'll know which ones are for you and for how long you should continue—and whether you'd be best served by choosing more. You may find, as I did, that you're wise to keep going with those that are most potent for you for months or even years.

Unlike some affirmations, words of power aren't lopsided promises of happily ever after. They're balanced, inspiring statements of true possibilities that utilize the treasures of your mind to help you materialize what you'd most love.

Words of Power

I am a genius, and I apply my wisdom.

I have a photographic mind with an infinite shutter speed.

I am wise, for I know that love
is the answer to all questions.

The light of wisdom guides me, and
the love of wisdom lifts me.

I have access to the wisdom of the ages.

I am present; and my mind is clear, sharp, and focused.

I have wisdom, for I am the light of my soul.

→ CHAPTER TWO ←

Immortality: Your Physical Treasures

"The human body is the best picture of the human soul."
— Ludwig Wittgenstein

The ship where I make one of my homes, *The World,* was docked in Dublin, Ireland, when a lovely lady, petite and sprightly, dressed impeccably and wearing a beautiful smile as her best accessory, walked into the ship's lobby and demanded, "Where's the party? Where's the action?"

All eyes followed her as she crossed the room and approached our social table. With a playful look, she again asked no one in particular, "Which young men will be taking me to the theater this evening?"

She turned her attention to me and inquired directly, "Are *you* available?" Naturally, I was curious and interested. There was something extraordinary about this woman. So I looked over at my special someone and asked her with a questioning nod if it was all right, and she said it was.

With my lady love's agreement, I escorted this dynamic woman to the theater that night. She held me in thrall, talking about how she'd just returned from Africa, where she'd climbed to the top of Mount Kilimanjaro. We had a great time, and she laughed at most of my jokes, giving me a knowing look and a naughty giggle for many of them.

About 10:30 that evening when the show was over, she said, enthusiastically, "Now can you all take me to a dance club?"

She was still going strong, but it was time for me to go back to the ship. So I declined, allowing the other two fellows who were with us to take her dancing. (She'd invited three of us because, she said, one man was rarely enough for her.) As we said good night, I told her that I was looking forward to meeting again on the ship. I hoped we could get to know each other better and was eager to hear more about her amazing adventures.

Indeed, she had a lot to tell me. *She was 94 years young.*

As we talked off and on over the next few days, I learned how much she still loved life and was truly fulfilling the promise of her "golden" years. She had dreams—places to go, people to meet, things to do—that kept her vital and grateful to be alive. She was an inspiration to meet and an example of what is humanly possible.

Your Physical Treasure #1: Vitality

Have you ever been just sitting around, doing little or nothing, feeling as if that's all the activity you can muster up, and you haven't even showered because it just feels like too much work? But then someone calls—someone important to you—and invites you to do something, and suddenly you have the energy to get up and go? You're inspired about what the day holds as you lather, rinse, dry, dress, and hurry on your way to meet this person!

That's just one example of how the body's reserves of energy rally the minute you have a compelling reason to get up off the couch. People who appear to live scattered, distracted, depressed, or repressed lives are often "suffering" from what seems to be a lack of inspiration. Think about the woman in the story you just read. She wasn't energized because she'd "made it" to 94; she was energized because she was *inspired* by what her life still held, by what was still to come.

In the first chapter of this book, you read about Paul Bragg, another example of continued vibrant health into old age. One of the many gifts he gave me was the idea that I needed to make a master plan for my life up to the age of 120. He said that I might as well plan to be doing something if I ever wanted to live to do it. He encouraged me to write my plan down in as much detail as possible—and never throw it away. I was to read and update it often. I've followed his advice, and as I write this now, I'm a little more than two years ahead of my original design, still writing and revising, still making plans for my 120th birthday.

Someone who sets a goal to run one mile will slow down at the first mile marker—but a marathoner is just warming up at that point. So, too, if you set your sights on living for a century and a quarter, then instead of slowing down, you'll just be hitting your stride as you approach your 75th year.

Look ahead to blowing out 120 candles.

I'm fond of saying that if you don't have a reason to live, you have a reason to die. People who have a will to live will live a long time. So if living a long, fulfilling life is important to you, you're wise to write down whatever you'd love to be, do, and have on your 70th, 100th, and 120th birthdays. Then do as Paul Bragg counseled me: Never throw this list away, review and update it often, and celebrate the progress you make as you age. Instead of feeling as if the advancing years are a burden, you can revel in the ageless beauty of a life well lived. You can count each year as a priceless addition to your physical treasury.

Your Physical Treasure #2: Longevity

Although living a long, full life requires that you have a vision for your future and set meaningful goals, there's no guarantee. The physical body can become diseased without warning; it can depart this life unexpectedly. Yet these facts of mortal existence don't alter the profound truths of your potentially immortal mental essence or soul.

You can choose to be connected to this essence in your lifetime, experiencing inspired consciousness. You can feel this at work as you produce something that will outlive your physical form. Many people feel this as they raise their children. Others find it in professional pursuits, having that sense of legacy in the books, buildings, art, wealth, or any number of other long-lasting creations people can leave behind to extend their lives by carrying the spirit forward after a physical death.

When your impact extends beyond your physical lifetime, you express your immortal essence. When you connect with that soulful essence in everyday life, you promote your perpetual youthfulness right now. And although there's no ironclad promise of longevity, you can do many things to enhance your well-being and vitality while you're here—all of which put the odds in your favor for a longer life.

Breathe deeply, using your diaphragm.

From your first inspiring inhalation at mortal birth to the last expiring exhalation at mortal death, you breathe. You couldn't live more than a few minutes without breath.

When you take long breaths in and let short ones out, you're emotionally elated. When you take short breaths in and let long ones out, you're emotionally depressed. When you have a balanced ratio of inhalation and exhalation, you're centered, poised, and in a grateful state of love. Balanced breath connects you with limitless, immortal spirit, while imbalanced breath keeps you rooted in the perceived limitations of your more transient mortal nature.

For centuries, this knowledge has ruled the rituals of those who knew how to use the breath to bring balance to daily living and extend their productive, meaningful lives. They knew to keep a rhythm—a musical harmony or proportion—with their breath.

To awaken your immortal, love-filled, healing nature, follow the breathing ritual below. Try it first thing in the morning or last thing at night. Five minutes is sufficient to experience its invigorating effects.

1. Breathe deeply through your nose, using your diaphragm. (If you're using your diaphragm, your belly will expand and contract with each inhalation and exhalation.)

2. Make your breath even. Take equal time with each breath in and each breath out.

3. Alternate between slow and quick respirations.

4. Breathe alternately and equally through the right and left nostrils.

It's a tenet of yoga that when the breath wanders, the mind is unsteady, but when the breath is still, the mind is calmed. In other words, mind follows breath. When you've mastered your breath, you will also have mastered your mind. And when you've mastered your mind, you will have liberated the source of your immortality.

Rest sufficiently: Sleep and meditate.

Rest allows time for bodily repair. When you're actively using your body, you gradually break it down. Without recuperation, you'd destroy the body, but it has a self-sustaining sleep-control system that automatically encourages you to stop and rest. **Listen to your body and follow its lead as to how much sleep you need.**

The more love and gratitude you have for life, the less you may need to rest, but when your daily emotional illusions have been running strong, there's nothing like a great rest period to realign yourself with the soulful truth. A catnap can do wonders for creative thoughts, and a moment of gratitude can refresh the body as well as the mind.

Use rest periods to clear away brain noise and repair the wearing tissues. Discover how much rest you need; sometimes, more sleep can make you sluggish and less sleep can make you yawn. Pay attention to what works for you, and experiment with different times. It may be that you need one long night's sleep, or you might need many short naps. Do what works for you.

One way to ensure that you're adequately rested is to supplement your sleep with meditation. This practice, which is basically just turning off the mental chatter while you remain awake, has been a proven stress reducer, helping your body to deal with—and in many cases heal—such conditions as chronic pain, headaches, anxiety, PMS, sleep disorders, and even infertility.

The simplest form of meditation is for you to sit or lie down (sitting makes it less likely you'll nod off, but if you're more comfortable reclining, do that), close your eyes, and pay attention to your breath. Breathe evenly and as you inhale, say to yourself, *In.* As you exhale, inwardly say, *Out.* If thoughts distract you momentarily, that's okay. Observe them like clouds floating by, and then go back to your breath. Most people start by meditating for about 5 minutes, building up over many sessions to 20 or 30 minutes at a time. Meditation is a treasure that puts you in tune with the universe.

Drink plenty of water.

Water is the universal solvent—if there's a fountain of youth, you can probably find it right there in your own kitchen. Your body is mostly water, which continually flushes, refreshes, and lubricates your body to keep it youthful. Without water, your physical body would stop working in just a few days.

When your brain and body are lubricated, so is your mind. And when your mind works freely, you're more receptive to universal "broadcasts," as the stations your brain attunes to operate on a higher frequency. The electrical nature of your soul-mind can more easily superconduct in your body when it's awash in water.

Drink at least a quart of water daily. Don't let yourself get too thirsty. By that point, you're already dehydrated. *Drink more water.*

Drink fresh, sun-ripened fruit and vegetable juices whenever you can.

Fresh fruit and vegetables are gifts from the gods. When they're sun ripened, they're filled with subtle organized electric fields that add to your own fields of life. The sun organizes the water molecules, adding a vibration and vitality to food that no other source can offer. Live, sun-ripened foods are storehouses of nutrients and flavors that refresh our minds and bodies. They've captured the sun's life-giving force and have converted it into a consumable fuel for living.

The life-giving elements of plants are the primaries of the food chain. When plants and their fruits are juiced, they're condensed. They become highly concentrated nutrient sources, packed with living enzymes and tingling elements that boost your energy. And when your energy is at its peak, you're most likely to receive and act on your highest inspirations and ideas.

Drink a glass of fresh fruit or vegetable juice at least once a week. Daily is even better. If you don't have access to a juicer, chew your food thoroughly to maximally extract the life-vibrating juice. However, it's wise to consume naturally sweet fruit or vegetable juices in moderation: the amount you'd normally consume when eating them raw and not juiced. High quantities of sweet fruit or vegetable juices can raise the glycemic index and initiate volatility in blood-sugar levels. Moderation is the key.

Eat what you love.
Be in love when you eat.

Love is the great food tonic. One of the wisest things you can do for your physical well-being is to love what you eat or eat what you love—and eat when you feel loved. But don't confuse *love for* food with *addiction to* food. Addiction is a perception of bottomless need, a feeling of craving and longing that can't be satisfied by anything but the object of your obsession. Love, on the other hand, is a balanced appreciation for all that food does for you. It's understanding how it can be either a benefit or a drawback and making wise choices directed by your own intuition and inspiration.

Your attitude has a major impact on your digestive processes. If you don't appreciate and love your food, you can contribute to its incomplete metabolism and even toxicity. Love and appreciation for a food enhances the food's vibrations and relaxes the body, which helps it more easily digest and assimilate the transformed food.

Don't force yourself to eat "health" foods if you're repelled by their flavor. Wheatgrass juice may indeed be a formidable detoxifier, for example, but if you're gulping it down and rejecting every minute of it, you're defeating the purpose of drinking it in the first place since your repulsion will make whatever you put into your belly toxic. Choose natural foods that you love, that enhance your well-being and invigorate your palate.

Loving your food naturally leads to gratitude for it. Human physiology functions best when it's in a state of love and thanksgiving. Your senses and muscles work optimally when you're in this state, and your brain and heart have coherent and relaxing waves. Even your cells become attuned to greater well-being.

Either eat the foods you love or learn to love the foods you eat, and begin each meal with a sincere expression of gratitude. Say it inwardly or outwardly, in whatever language rings true for you. You might say thanks for the sustenance, the life-giving energy of the food; the plant(s) or the animal(s) who may have given their lives for your benefit; and the people who grew, harvested, and prepared the food.

Eat fresh greens, grains, fish, and fowl.
Eat moderately, especially at night.

A balance of the essential nutrients is wise, of course. Fresh greens, grains, fish, and fowl have been the sound basics for centuries. Just as with investing, it's not healthy to focus on only a few things; you're wise to diversify. Eat a balance of basic, wholesome foods.

Being fanatical about your food is also unwise. There's nothing wrong with a short-term dietary restriction or addiction, but over time, those narrow parameters would eventually hinder your overall well-being.

Along those same lines, practice moderation in quantity. Habitually undereating to the point of malnourishment is just as hard on your body as habitually overeating to the point of excess. For those who have a tendency to eat too little, they're wise to remember how much energy is derived from food and how vital this energy is to every cell in the body. For those who have a tendency to eat too much, they're wise to remember that the extra food will literally weigh them down, making them sluggish and adding pounds. The lymphatic system backs up after consuming a heavy meal, particularly one rich in fat and protein.

Practice moderation in your relationship with food. Love it, eat it, and leave it when you're sated. You can help your body digest better and maximize the energy from your food if you eat about the same amount of food each day at about the same time each day. For most people, eating larger portions earlier in the day and lighter portions toward the evening is optimal, but it's best to find and follow your own inner rhythm.

Spend 15 minutes in the sun a few days each week.

Even though you've been warned against overexposure to the sun, this doesn't mean that you must stay out of the sun completely. A little exposure is vital for health, particularly to help your body naturally create vitamin D.

The sun offers you a special vibration that you can't receive from any other source. As it provides life essence to flora, so too does it provide life essence to fauna, as its source of power helps organize the very molecules of your living cells.

Just as the ancient sun worshippers bowed in awe and respect before the morning sun, it would be wise for you to not only watch a beautiful, colorful sunrise, but also to acknowledge the sun for being such a gift to you. **Thank the sun daily for being the source of energy for life. Spend up to 15 minutes in the sun a few days each week, whether or not you exercise outside.**

Do the seven life-empowering exercises.

It can be fun to take up the latest exercise craze, but there are also a few exercises that have been with us since the beginning. They've withstood the test of time, and you're wise to participate in these as your health permits.

1. **Walking.** Walk at least a mile a day.

2. **Running (or rapid walking).** Run for ten minutes once a week.

3. **Swimming.** Swim for ten minutes as often as possible.

4. **Dancing.** Dance alone or with others whenever you can.

5. **Climbing.** Find some incline, whether it's stairs, bleachers, a treadmill, a hill, and so on. Climb at least once a week.

6. **Making love.** There may be a limit on this exercise, but I haven't found it. Do this when your love prevails.

7. **Stretching.** Stretch your joints to their fullest range every day. Exhale as you flex, and inhale as you extend.

Work up a sweat at least three times a week.

Your body is covered by your largest organ: your skin. It's full of microscopic kidneylike structures called sweat glands that can become congested if they're not used to capacity on occasion. Skin also breathes; and when the skin's breathing structures aren't occasionally being used to their fullest potential, they can become blocked, too. Taking care of your skin is essential for optimal functioning, so open it up through exercise or, alternately, by being in a hot environment (either outdoors or in a sauna or steam shower). You can imagine this as a time for opening the channels of your soul and contemplating your dreams while you truly open yourself up to the world around you.

Your Physical Treasure #3: Self-Healing

Every cell in your body serves to fulfill your dreams. Every part of you reminds you to love, serves as your teacher, and speaks out to you in the form of symptoms that guide you to greater levels of awareness. When your body feels sick, it's speaking to you; and if you know how to listen carefully, your body will help you normalize physical, emotional, and mental imbalances.

Whenever any part of your body is "unhealthy," the resulting symptoms and signs reflect a conflict between your mind-body perceptions and your soul's loving and immortal wisdom. Symptoms and warning signs are reminders inviting you to resolve this conflict and encouraging you to release whatever illusions you cling to about your reality—and whatever exaggerations or minimizations you've made about your existence.

See your chiropractor.

Since ancient times, wise "healers" have looked to the spine for the sake of enhancing well-being, realizing that if the spine isn't aligned, life cannot be expressed to the fullest. If there are misalignments in the spine, there are corresponding misalignments in the mind. The original objective of aligning or adjusting the spine was to reconnect the physical self with the soul by aligning the mortal spine—the lifeline—to the immortal source of life and health.

The term *subluxation* used by chiropractors today originated from three Latin roots: *sub,* or less than; *lux,* as in divine light or intelligence; and *ation,* which means "a condition of." So the word implies a mortal condition of less than divine immortal light and full expression.

Chiropractic adjustments realign your mortal self with your immortal self, reconnecting you physically and spiritually. When I was a practicing chiropractor, I used to say, "I align spines and minds with the Divine and make people feel fine!" When you've connected mortal with immortal, you're in sync with the universe, which helps your body return to greater well-being and maintain peak performance. It allows you to receive greater quantities of the mysterious breath of life.

Realize that your body works for you, not against you.

What's amazing to me is that somehow in our society, we've gotten the idea that disease is bad! I want to break that down and share something different with you. In working with thousands of people in clinical cases, my observation is that when a person experiences disease, the body is simply attempting to deliver a message that will enable that person to make corresponding lifestyle and perceptual adjustments and thus live to his or her full potential. Sometimes the signs and symptoms we think of as diseases are actually feedback mechanisms that can help us.

I realize that we haven't completely figured out the complex interactions and communications between the mind and body. We don't yet have all this nailed down as a science. Decoding these messages of the body is a highly personal pursuit right now, but I believe that in the future—in the decades to come—we'll uncover these secrets and become more adept at reading the messages of the body. In time, this will help us prevent so-called diseases from advancing. When we can catch diseases in their earliest, subtlest phases and alter our perceptions before they break down the body, "health care" will certainly be completely revolutionized.

Meanwhile, the body attempts to guide us to live more fully, to live in alignment with our spiritual selves and immortal knowing. The most remarkable treasure of the body is its ability to be whole in a state of well-being. Just as you have the power to create the cells of your body, you have the power to heal the cells of your body. You have the ability to transform "disease" and bring "healing." Love and gratitude are the greatest "healers."

Anything that you stress about—anything that you don't uncover and dissolve by identifying its hidden gift—is automatically stored in your body and can be felt in the form of signs and symptoms. Whenever you have an imbalanced perspective about the universe and see disorder, you're either attracted or repelled. You like or dislike; you experience pleasure or pain. Whatever you polarize your perceptions about in this way affects your cells in the same way, causing tension and compression in the cells that could be considered a state of disorder. It causes too much or too little activity of the cell—which we currently call disease. These very same polarizations also communicate imbalances to the brain, causing further emotional reactions, which then go to the cells and impose even more tension and compression. It's a cycle of reflexes and consciousness.

A man once came halfway across the U.S. to a program I held in Houston, Texas. His body was covered with psoriasis, and it was concentrated over his joints and part of his face. His psoriasis had begun in his childhood and hadn't let up since. As he worked through The Demartini Method at my seminar, The Breakthrough Experience, he had to find the hidden order in the apparent chaos of his life. When he completed the program, he was brought to tears, feeling so much love for a father whom he'd alienated since he was a child—around the same time that his psoriasis had started. This man had thought of his father as mean and violent and had harbored deep anger for him, avoiding him for years.

Yet when he found a way to love his father and see him from a different perspective, the man's skin started to transform. He realized that in the depths of his soul, he wanted to love his dad, as all people do. This was a catharsis for him.

Within three days, some of his lesions started to calm, and within a week, his inflamed skin started to return to pink. In the next two weeks, his psoriasis was gone. This physical manifestation of his irritation had served its purpose once the man returned to love.

Choose to view any "disease" as a gift, a direct communication from the immortal self to the mortal self. Remember that the signs and symptoms of the body give you feedback to try to guide your mind's awareness and your body's actions back to poise and balance, to love and gratitude.

Love and thank every part of your body.

Any part of your body that doesn't receive your love and gratitude functions less effectively: Without these two essential and balanced feelings, your body can't fully guide and serve you.

When you think about a particular part of your body, that part receives added blood and nourishment. When you love and are grateful for this part of you, it receives even more vital elements. If you're interested in staying for a while in this body, show love and gratitude for every part of it.

While you're honoring your miraculous body, be sure to show the same love and gratitude to the source that created it. No mortal human being at this stage of conscious evolution has sufficient intelligence to organize and manage a single cell, let alone an entire physical body. It's time that we acknowledge the creative intelligence that governs our genetics and organizes and maintains our bodies. What a magnificent universe our body inhabits! What a magnificent experience love is! You're wise to show more love and gratitude to the creative and transformative intelligence of your body. Thank your inner creative intelligence for your amazing mortal creation with all its wonderfully coordinated parts.

Words of Power

Love is the greatest of all healers.

Every cell of my body is filled with love.

My vitality, stamina, and tone are phenomenal.

I have endurance, and I am vibrant.

My energy and inner state of well-being are astounding.

I am moderate, rhythmic, and consistent.

I love and am grateful for my body—what a masterpiece!

CHAPTER THREE

Divinity: Your Spiritual Treasures

"What is god, what is not god, what is between man
And god, who shall say?"
— Euripides

Imagine the soul as an everlasting, infinite vibration stretching endlessly. Envision it reaching out to the infinity of divinity and coming back to touch the "fininity" of humanity through the workings of its extended and intelligent mind. Envision the soul as the interim between these two—the junction point between unity and individuality, between the divine and the human, between the infinite and the finite.

Most of the great spiritual traditions teach this underlying idea that the soul connects our mortal selves with the immortal divine. Regardless of the particular belief, religion, or practice, this fundamental understanding proves similar. I once heard this idea described as a candle in a multicolored lantern, and although each of us may peer at the light through a different-hued pane of glass, we're all seeing the same flame.

When you look deeply and delve into the secret treasures inside your heart where love lives, it's possible to realize that everything is worthy of love, and ultimately, everything is an expression of spirituality. Why limit our spirituality only to our luminous, expansive essence? Sometimes I hear people say, "He's not spiritual" about someone else, or they proudly announce about themselves: "I'm a spiritual person." Let me confront you with something here: *Who isn't spiritual?* Even if you don't identify yourself with organized religion or any particular practice, I'd maintain that you're still a spiritual person with spiritual pursuits. *Where is spirituality not? Where is love not?*

Many theologians have written about the omnipresence of divinity and/or spirituality and that you can find it, for example, in a blade of grass or at a supermarket just as readily as in a mosque, temple, or church. In his book *Out of My Later Years,* Albert Einstein wrote: "If this Being [God] is omnipotent, then every occurrence, including every human action, every human thought, and every human feeling and aspiration is also His work." In other words, if we're going to acknowledge that there's a "Grand Organized Design" (GOD) in this universe—and Einstein did—then it follows that everything we do, think, feel, and aspire to all exist as part of that design.

When I began studying morals and ethics, I discovered something fascinating: Whatever you believe, you can find an opposite set of beliefs somewhere in the world. Whatever you stand for, someone else stands against it. What's so great about that? You might think about it like arm wrestling: As two people pit their strengths against one another, each grows from it. When you realize that other people have their own values and spiritual ideals and that this actually helps you strengthen your own, you might find yourself more able to honor and embrace those who believe something different from you.

Once when I was in El Salvador, I saw a parade of people dressed in white, blue, and other bright colors. They were dancing, playing music, and celebrating at a fever pitch. What was the occasion? It was a funeral, but they weren't mourning—they were rejoicing the passing of a mortal body into a spiritual domain. What a completely different view of things than we experience most places in the United States! And I think there's something to be learned from that—and from every chance we have to look at the light through a new color.

The Greatest Spiritual Treasure: Your Spiritual Quest

Ultimately, each one of us experiences spirituality according to our individual values. In other words, if your highest value is your family and your children, then you'll feel that your highest calling is to raise a magnificent family. President Kennedy's mother, Rose, provided an obvious example when she said, "I looked at child rearing not only as a work of love and duty, but as a profession that was fully as interesting and challenging as any honorable profession in the world, and one that demanded the best that I could bring to it." Raising her children was her spiritual quest.

Your spiritual quest can be *anything* based on your higher values. No two people have the exact same values, so no two people have the same idea of what spirituality is. Each soul-mind expresses itself in its singular way. I like to think of it in this way: As the higher energy frequency lowers or descends to the finiteness of humanity, it dualizes into a value system and animates or incarnates into a body. Each physical incarnation and each value system, comprising "positives" and "negatives," has the imprint of God *and* the unique expression of an individual.

Whatever you love and dedicate your life to shows you where your spirituality and even your spiritual quest can be found. I can imagine that Donald Trump's spiritual life might revolve around building giant, first-class structures in New York, Atlantic City, or other major cities across the globe. My own is all about traveling as a teacher, healer, and philosopher, setting foot in every country throughout the world. I feel this is my GOD-ordained gift—the reason I'm here on this planet.

Do you know what your values are? Do you have a sense of your spiritual mission?

If you don't and I've got you thinking, we're right on track. If you'd like some help discovering your own values, that's coming up. Meanwhile, let me advise you again to remain aware of what an illusion it is to judge someone else's values—or even your own—as wrong. It's not uncommon for someone to react to my description of Trump's spirituality with some kind of sneer: "That's not spiritual. That's just materialism, pride, and greed." Or you fill in the blank with whatever pejorative word you might use. But please realize that no one's values are "wrong," and no one else's are "right." (Although everyone at times thinks theirs *are* "right.")

This concept seems especially difficult for people where money is concerned—it's one of the main reasons why I wrote the book *How to Make One Hell of a Profit and Still Get to Heaven.* In it, I addressed the nature of the spiritual and material, including how many people perceive them as if they were oil and water and never mix. Yet I see no reason these two human driving forces can't be integrated—they aren't at odds with each other.

The ancient Egyptians said that spirit without matter is expressionless, and matter without spirit is motionless. The two together make up existence as we know it. When the two are separated, we're disempowered. When they're united, we have true power—we experience wholeness. Hubert Howe Bancroft, a historian and publisher, once proposed that if we can marry our spiritual drive and our material drive—if we can achieve our spiritual cause and receive material wealth in the process, and in turn use our material wealth for that spiritual cause—then we are the greatest power on the planet. He pointed out that all the people, institutions, and cultures that have left a profound imprint on the world have done so because they've integrated these two forces.

This is just to ask again, *Where is spirit not? Where is love not?* It's everywhere, in everything, and in everyone.

Ever since I was 17 and had my near-death experience (the accidental strychnine poisoning I mentioned earlier), I've felt a desire to understand health, wholeness, well-being, and human potential. So I've dedicated my life to that—it's my spiritual quest. In the second chapter, you also read about my "mission book," which was inspired by Paul Bragg's admonition to write down my purpose and objectives, review them constantly, update them regularly, and never throw them away. What began on a scrap of paper many years ago has become a series of large books and a daily reading ritual: Every day

I work on it, refining my mission and my dreams. Right now, my mission and dream books include four volumes describing every single thing I'd love to create in my life spiritually, mentally, vocationally, financially, socially, physically, and in my family.

You see, once I realized that *if I don't decide, someone else decides,* I made a commitment to put my heart and soul into this creation. If you read what I've written there, it would be obvious to you that I've poured thousands of hours of work into it. No doubt I've spent more time on this than on anything else in my life.

Let me encourage you to use this book to spur you into beginning and evolving your own mission book. You can create a notebook, computer file, or what have you, and you can record your responses to all the questions you read here. Creating this type of document for yourself will not only give you a greater sense of connection with your spiritual purpose, but it will help you clarify it to such an extent that you can see, feel, hear, and taste every aspect of it.

Once your mind is clear and your heart is open, magic happens and the universe seems to lay out a red carpet for you to get where you're headed. If you're not sure about your intentions, you probably have to work like hell to get whatever you nebulously imagine you're after. Know this: Whatever you write down as your spiritual pathway will open doors. Some people may dismiss this, but you'll never be able to convince me that writing down your dreams isn't incredibly powerful. That's because it isn't just an idea that I like to talk about but never do myself. No! I've watched the power of my dreams unfolding as I've written about them in my mission book.

And I advocate that you do the same for yourself. This has inspired me, and I'd love to help you live an inspired life of your own in your own unique way. So I ask you again to explore this with depth, seriousness, clarity, and inspiration: What is your spiritual purpose, your cause, your immortal quest? What is your service to the world? What do you want to contribute? What is your hidden spiritual agenda—that is, what do you want in return for your service? Find your spiritual mission—whatever it is! Find out what truly inspires you, and start defining exactly what you'd love in your life.

Start by discovering your values. What follows over the next several pages is an abbreviated version of the values discussion in Chapter 3 of my book *The Heart of Love.* You have all that you need here to determine your own values system, but if you find that you'd like to explore this subject in greater depth, as well as learn how to connect with other people through *their* values system, I recommend you read that book, too.

Your values can be expressed in all—or just a few—of the seven areas of life: *spiritual, mental, vocational, financial, familial, social,* and *physical.* Each is equally valid as an avenue for achieving a deeply fulfilling connection with the universe. Yet sometimes people allow their fears to keep them from being *aware* that they're living according to their values, and this can cause stress and a sense of emptiness. They let the opinions of others and the judgments they have about themselves cause them to think that they "should" have certain other value systems. As you complete this exercise on discovering your values, see if you can let go of "should" and get to what's really true for you.

1. How Do You Fill Your Space?

Investigate the places where you spend the most time. Pretend you've never been there before; and identify themes, common elements, and evidence of your values. Whatever is prevalent in your living, working, and recreational spaces gives you the first clue to your values.

Think figuratively. A home filled with photos doesn't necessarily mean an appreciation for photography. (What's pictured: family members, travel destinations, architecture, something else?) Ask yourself, *What do these things that I've chosen to surround myself mean to me?*

2. How Do You Spend Your Time?

Take a look at how you allocate your waking hours. What claims most of your day? What comes in second? Third? Fourth? The list may not identically parallel your values, but it will come close. Most people spend the lion's share of the day at work. Depending on your occupation (and how much you love it or not), this can mean that you have any number of values at the top of your list: financial security, creativity, contribution—whatever it is that working gives to you. A doctor may work because health/healing is her highest value, or maybe it's intellect or wealth. Who can say? Only the doctor. Think about *why* you work so much at your profession.

If you don't spend most of your time on work, what do you do with the day? Is it raising a family, doing volunteer work, playing golf, socializing, or campaigning for a cause? Whatever you devote the most time to is likely to reflect your highest value.

However, your time is only one indicator that you can combine with all the others as you answer the rest of the questions to help you figure out your real values. In other words, if you look at what you're prioritizing in terms of time and then view those things in consideration of the other ten categories coming up, your values will begin to come into sharp focus.

Note: It's possible that you may feel as if your time isn't always being spent doing what you love or doing what's truly in alignment with your highest values. When this perception occurs, you may feel as if your life is stressful. But ultimately it's impossible *not* to live according to your values since all of your decisions are based upon what you imagine will fulfill your highest values with the most advantages at any one moment. It's quite possible that security or even the desire to please or fit in has trumped your other values for a time. If you have the sense that you've structured your actions around what someone else thinks your values *should* be just because you want to please them, fit in, or possibly because of a desire for security, then ask yourself, *How else would I spend my time if I had none of these fears or concerns?*

3. How Do You Spend Your Energy?

Think about what you *love* doing for long periods of time. What are you doing when you lose track of time? Where is your "attention surplus order"?

You certainly have plenty of energy to perform those actions you value most because doing what you love energizes you. Like everyone else, you become fatigued easily when you can't see how something that you're doing will fulfill your highest values—and completely juiced when you can see that it does. For example, if you can't focus on an Internet research project for work yet can surf sports Websites for hours, that's a reflection of your values. (Or if you still haven't called your parents about their upcoming visit but you've responded to all your work e-mails—even the jokes—that's also a clear indicator.)

Ask yourself, *For what actions do I seem to have plenty of energy? What actions invigorate me? Where do I love to spend the most energy during the day, the week, or the month?*

4. How Do You Spend Your Money?

Look to see how you use money in your life. Do you squirrel it away? Are you an investor? A risk taker? Do you spend lots of cash on clothes, education, or travel? Do you throw lavish parties, keep your money to yourself, or donate to charities? Are you saving for specifics, such as your children's education, retirement, or buying a prize-winning pig or a 50-foot yacht? Does most of your spending occur in the realm of business, home, community, or something else?

Simply put, where does it all go? As they say, follow the money. It leaves a trail you can follow straight to your values.

5. Where Are You Most Organized?

Your highest value will be the most ordered area of your life, with little or no chaos. There's greater chaos in the area of your lower values, so other people tend to control you in these areas. Your lowest values will require outside motivation to force you to pay attention and get things done in this area. Is your garden manicured but your checkbook's a mess? Is your garage workshop a disaster but your desk and files at work are immaculate?

Ask yourself, *Where's the greatest order in my life? Where do things run most smoothly with the least amount of volatility?* This reveals your highest value. *Where is the greatest chaos? Where do things seem unpredictable and erratic?* This reveals the lower values.

6. Where Are You Most Disciplined?

Consider the areas in which you're most consistent, diligent, and conscientious. Nobody has to get you up in the morning to do the actions that are truly most important to you. You can easily focus on and remain disciplined and steady on that which you truly care about. Whenever you unwisely label yourself as "not focused" or "undisciplined," it's because there's something else higher on your value hierarchy vying for your attention, and you're expecting yourself to live otherwise.

What are you engaged in when you're consistently focused and disciplined?

7. What Do You Think About?

When your mind wanders, where does it go? Your values tend to interrupt your regularly scheduled programming. You'll be having lunch with a friend and thoughts of something other than what's on the menu—both figuratively and literally—will pop up. You may find yourself thinking about work even when you're at home, or vice versa. If you're frequently distracted by thoughts of one thing while you're involved with something else, what are those intruding thoughts? They probably have something to do with your higher values.

Then again, you may spend a good part of your day consciously choosing to think about certain things. Your vocation or your avocation may cause you to focus on specific topics for hours at a time. What are you constantly mulling over, considering, and trying to understand even more?

In the Bible, Solomon declares: "As a man thinketh in his heart, so is he." Look to your thoughts and learn who you are.

8. What Do You Visualize?

Explore your dreams and visions. What do you see for yourself? What is your vision for your life, your future? When you daydream and envision yourself unreservedly loving your life, what is the recurring theme?

9. What Do You Talk to Yourself About?

Like everyone else, you have self-talk. Sometimes it builds you up and sometimes it tears you down, but all of your self-talk ultimately hones you in on what's most important. You even have an internal dialogue, where parts of you converse with other parts. **What are those conversations about?**

You may debate actions you "should" take . . . what kind of actions do you discuss with yourself? You may evaluate other people or opportunities; and you may weigh your skills and talents, making lists of pros and cons about any variety of things. You may make plans for yourself or your family, your home or your business ventures, or your next vacation. What's the subject of your internal banter?

Internally, you're constantly discussing with yourself what's really most important: what you really would love to manifest and create in your life. You're constantly running affirmations or words of power through your mind, both constructive and destructive, and these color and even generate your perceptions in life. All of these internal dialogues revolve and oscillate around your highest values.

10. What Do You Talk about with Others?

Eavesdrop on your own conversations. When you meet someone new, what do you find yourself chatting about most? When you're with old friends, what topics do you revisit time and again? What conversations captivate you and keep you interested for the longest period of time? Pay close attention to whatever you keep leading your conversations toward.

11. What Do You React To?

Pay attention to what you pay attention to. Notice what makes you smile and frown, and what causes you to lean in to hear more or fold your arms in front of your body and shut down. Stay aware, and this kind of emotional feedback will serve you in getting to know yourself incredibly well.

12. What Are Your Goals?

If you're a person who writes down goals and works toward them, simply consult your current list of objectives. Do they all revolve around business? Or family? Or vacations? Do you see a pattern here, too?

It's a pretty direct correlation. People who have financial values high on their list will have income goals, investing goals, retirement goals, acquisition goals, and so on. People who possess mental values will have academic goals, intellectual-achievement goals, skill-acquisition goals, and so forth. High vocational values will evoke goals in career advancement and professional acknowledgment, while physical values will inspire goals concerning body fat, blood chemistry, athletic accomplishment, and the like. Spiritual, familial, and social values express themselves in typical goal-oriented fashion also, especially for those who have these areas highest on their list of values.

Goals of higher importance are generally demonstrated by being written faster and more fluently, having clearer details and broader content, being easier to read, and inspiring tears.

If you don't have written objectives, **simply consider what you would most love to do, be, or have in your life, and which of those goals you are actively moving toward.** Which ones do you pursue nearly every day?

Reflecting on Your Values and Connecting with Your Spiritual Purpose

Now you probably have a greater sense of your values and their hierarchy, and which ones are most and least important to you. If you haven't done it already, I suggest that you write down your answers to the 12 questions I've posed, and take the time to rank your values, too. Then be sure to sit and reflect on what's there. Is what you've written in line with your everyday living? Have you identified and consciously chosen to pursue your spiritual quest, one that reflects your highest value?

Although I'm still relatively young, people ask me all the time why I don't retire. Forget retirement! Retirement is for people who haven't found their mission. Because I know and embrace my purpose, I can't imagine stopping everything I'm doing just because I've reached a certain financial or chronological milestone. Retirement is an artificial system—an arbitrary mind-set that Americans accepted in the 1930s. But it's not *truth*. In ancient times, farmers, craftspeople, philosophers, and leaders kept right on doing what they were doing—doing what they were great at—until death or ill health prevented them from it. The truth is somebody in her 90s climbing Mount Kilimanjaro, like the lady you read about in Chapter 2. The truth is an individual like Patricia Bragg, my initial mentor's daughter, who's still traveling the world serving people—just as her father did—well into a ripe, mature age. These are my heroes: the people who find their dreams and are dedicated and inspired to do something meaningful.

Each one of these people connect deeply with a spiritual purpose *in their own way.* As the poet Ralph Waldo Emerson wrote: "God enters by a private door into every individual." Through what door does the divine presence, by whatever name you call it, enter you?

If you'd like to become aligned more closely with your own spiritual purpose, engage in any, many, or all of the following practices—each are proven to help you connect regularly.

Center yourself in love.

People often say, "I just want to be happy." But the imbalanced emotion called *happiness* is just one of two outer masks that can be worn, both of which cover the true inner feeling called *love* that remains ever present within your heart. Even when you feel the imbalanced emotion called *sadness,* which is the other outer mask, you're actually experiencing a compensatory withdrawal symptom that results from your addiction to its counterpart labeled happiness with its unrealistic expectation(s). True love is profound, illuminated, poised—it's not excited, nor is it unrealistically expecting. It's full of impact, it's clear, and it's lucid. It transforms lives.

Our minds cling to the idea of happiness—it's a form of addiction. Look beyond your outer imbalanced mind and its emotional covering and zoom into your heart to see the greater truth. When you do, you'll have a balanced mind that naturally stands upright in gratitude. You don't have to "make" yourself thankful; it's just a state of being that happens when you center yourself in love.

It's only your imbalanced perceptions that can get in the way of your heart: "My life is hard right now," "I need a relationship to be happy," or "I'm too old to start saving for retirement." These things may seem true to you, but they're only half of the truth. You're wise to recognize the other complementary and opposite half, and then you'll have a profound opening to love. Try this exercise to see what I mean.

1. Divide your age by four. During the next four days, you'll review a quarter of your life per day. For example, if you're 48, then on the first day you'll be working on years 0 to 12; on the second day, it will be 13 to 24; and so on.

2. As you review the quarter each day, write down any moment when you see some kind of imbalance, either positive or negative. For example, someone was mean to you, you were lost, you didn't have enough money for something you wanted, or you had effortless success in some endeavor, someone praised you, or you were doing work you liked.

3. After you've written down the perceived imbalance each day, immediately work to

> find the counterbalancing event. Look for the opposite. You'll find it! Take your time and really consider the following: If someone was mean to you, who was nice? Dig until you find it. If you were lost, in what ways were you found? If you lacked money, where did you experience abundance? Similarly, if you experienced effortless success in some area, in what endeavor were you struggling? If you were praised, who was trying to tear you down? If you were doing work you liked, what chores did you have to do that weren't as fulfilling?

Do this over the four days and I promise that if you sincerely want to see the balance, you'll be able to. If you commit yourself to "getting it," you'll definitely be able to create a completely balanced list of events *for your entire life up until today.* That's because there is a balanced and hidden divine order. There is no true chaos, just the perception of chaos.

Upon carefully inspecting your life, you'll discover that your pains and pleasures bless you equally. Why is it important to see this? Because the essence of spirituality is the experience of love and gratitude for the greater designer and design, for the universe exactly as it exists. This love is born when you join your pains and pleasures as one. The balance of mind breeds the love of heart.

To take this insight even deeper, you're wise to further explore each painful moment of sorrow and find in it how it has blessed and served you, and how it has blessed and served others. Then consider each pleasurable moment of joy and find in it how it has not blessed and served you, and how it has not blessed and served others. Each event that you've identified—both difficult and easy, sorrowful and joyful—has indeed made a contribution to your life and the lives of others. Taking the time to acknowledge this puts you in a state of grateful love, the most powerful connection between you and spirit.

Expand your meditating mind.

In the previous chapter, you read about the benefits of meditation to rest the mind and supplement your sleep, but it's also highly regarded as a way of reconnecting with spirit—creating an inner communion where you can become poised and present and where you can learn.

Gratitude is the key that opens the gateway to your heart and allows the eternal love inside to come out into the world. When your heart is opened by gratitude and love, your mind becomes clear and inspired. Suddenly an inner voice comes to you; and both your physical body and mental state become enthusiastic, inspired, and ready to act on those visions and messages from within.

You might say that meditation of this type is about listening to this inner voice and seeing this inner vision. Prayer can be like talking to your self, having a dialogue with your innermost being. In this state of gratitude, you make some of the most magnificent decisions and receive some of the most creative insights. Genius runs free here, bestowing its gifts of great music, poetry, philosophy, art, and ideas in so many other areas, including business and finance.

Most people are constantly surrounded by opinions. Almost everyone you meet has an opinion they'd like to share, and nearly everyone projects their own values on to the world around them—including you. Certainly, you can learn from someone with a different set of values, but if you're not taking time to hear your own inner voice, you can buy into other people's values and become distracted from your own.

When the vision and the voice on the inside become greater than all the opinions on the outside, you've begun to master your life.

Follow these steps to commune with your higher guide, your inner voice. Hear it, listen to it, and follow its vision:

1. Stand relaxed with your hands loosely at your sides.

2. Take a few deep breaths, inhaling and exhaling through your nose.

3. Turn your head up 45 degrees.

4. Shift your gaze upward another 45 degrees until you're looking at the ceiling.

5. Close your eyes and relax your lids.

6. Think about everything for which you're thankful. Conduct a review of your whole life, and feel the gratitude in your body.

7. Keep thinking and thanking until you truly feel your heart open up and you release a tear (or several) of inspiration.

8. Upon attaining this state, ask your inner guide for any messages. Ask, *Inner voice, do you have a message for me at this moment?*

9. When you're grateful enough and ask sincerely, a message will come. Write it down.

10. Ask if there are any others. If so, write them down.

Put yourself in an inspiring or spiritual place.

We can awaken our inspired state when we come into contact with inspiring places, people, and creations. You may sense the inspiring divine presence in the great outdoors or in your own living room—of course, it can be found anywhere and everywhere. At the same time, you're wise to consciously seek out what inspires you; it's what puts you in touch with spirit. Consider these possibilities:

— **Visit the birthplaces of great spiritual leaders and other "sacred" sites and religious buildings, and meditate there.** By visiting, you may experience a unique presence of spiritual energy. Many of these places elicit a special reverence and calm, which evokes a broadening of appreciation and love. Performing the ancient ritual of meditation in such awe-inspiring centers of worship can cause you to desire a life of greater spiritual action. It will often make you expand your dreams or ambitions, motivating you to contribute something even more inspiring to humanity. Or your meditation may bring out a more awakened and loving nature from within. Journey into the realm of immortality, the heavenly planes of higher life, by visiting these masterpieces of architecture or imagining yourself in their halls or chambers.

— **Read inspirational works and study great teachers.** With the vastness of modern technology, there's no reason you can't immerse yourself in whatever tradition of wisdom that inspires you. Seek out writings that speak to you and illuminate your own understanding of the order in the universe. Read them and sift through their messages. Expose yourself to the biographies of the great teachers, as well as to their teachings. Imagine undergoing what these remarkable beings experienced by putting yourself in their shoes. Pretend you were in their spaces and times. Would you have the same dedication and inspiration to carry out your mission? Imagine if you did, and then imagine to what heights of greatness your life would soar.

— **Listen to sacred music.** One of the beautiful things about listening to music such as Gregorian chant, Buddhist bells, or Hindu raga is that you can feel as if you're swimming in sound—swimming in spirit. The resonance heals and moves body, mind, and spirit. Regardless of your religious affiliation or creed, the celebrated masterpieces of music will awaken a higher calling within you while uplifting you. Listen and you'll become more like those who inspired their creation. To hear the divine harmonies is to awaken your divine nature.

Record your inspirations and act on them.

Be sure to write down all of the inspiring ideas you encounter, as well as the ones that you create yourself. I've compiled a book called *The Philosophers of Wisdom,* in which I've extracted the greatest teachings of many of the most distinguished minds I've studied so far, both religious and otherwise. It also contains my reactions to these teachings, as well as the most creative and insightful thoughts I've had on my own. I can open the book to any page and be reinspired by what I've gathered there. *What speaks to you? What moves your soul?* Take the time to capture these inspirations so you'll have them with you anytime you want to reconnect with spirit.

When you receive messages from your own inner wisdom, be sure to follow them. You're designed to make your own life difficult whenever you don't respond to the intuitions and then inspirations of your own soul. This is the grand and magnificent design of evolution—not a problem, but a blessing. This assures you that no matter what happens, you're constantly guided (pressured, even) to evolve and gradually unfold your spiritual mission, talent, and destiny. When you feel like you're off purpose, life seems to get rocky and forces you to listen and look within . . . listen to the guide within.

Today we're finally emerging from what some have imagined to be an unenlightened era: For many decades, Western medicine has considered people who've heard the inner voice as "ill." But all the celebrated spiritual or other leaders listened to the wisdom of their true inner voice (as distinguished from "the voices") and awakened that special inner communion.

Each of the actions outlined in the book up to this point have helped awaken you to your ever-present inner spirit. When you have the four pillars of self-mastery—gratitude, love of the heart, certainty, and presence of the mind—then I don't think there's anything on this planet that can't be summoned into your life. We're here as intentional creators to manifest forms from matter and energy. Whoever awakens the most certainty manifests the forms most effectively, and whoever has the most self-worth manifests the grandest forms most directly. We have access to this—and that's everyone's spiritual quest. When you consciously participate in the fashioning of the universe, you walk hand in hand with the divine. You've found and consciously live your purpose.

Words of Power

I am a star, and I shine my loving radiance.

I am a magnificent being living in a magnificent universe.

I am an infinite being remembering to love in a finite world.

My soul is my heart's connection to my infinite source.

I am loving, I am grateful, and my life is blessed.

I am humble, I am a disciple, and I listen to my soul.

I am an expression of the divinity, and I honor myself.

CHAPTER FOUR

Wealth: Your Financial Treasures

"Riches serve a wise man but command a fool."
— English proverb

My debut in the world of professional speaking took place in my own apartment. I'd invited a group of people over to hear me talk, and I poured my heart into it. At the end, I thought my speech had been inspired and I'd done a great job—and sure enough, everyone congratulated me. "You're a natural!" they told me. "Keep it up!" they encouraged. "You'll go far!" they predicted.

After everyone left, I went to collect my financial rewards from the bowl I'd labeled "Love Donations." But when I looked inside, all I found was a lone $5 bill.

In that moment, I realized that even though I'd been thinking that all I wanted to do was give and spread the love by delivering my message, I'd also been hoping—unconsciously and perhaps unrealistically—that people would be so moved by my words that they'd drop some serious cash into the bowl.

All right, I admitted to myself, *I guess I would love to make some real money at this.*

So the next time I had people over to hear me speak, I put a label on the bowl that said, "Minimum Love Donation: $5." I also placed the bowl in a much more prominent spot in my living room.

Once again, I received wonderful encouragement from the people who came to listen, and this time, there were three $5 bills in the bowl. That qualified as a definite improvement, but it still wasn't even enough to keep the lights on in my apartment for the next month.

On the following attempt my label said, "Minimum Love Donation: $10," and the donation bowl remained front and center. At the end of my speech, I even mentioned that I'd appreciate contributions, and that day I collected a few $10 bills. Only a small number of people had "shared the love" in cash.

So I changed my label again, and this time it said, "Minimum Fee: $20." And that day, almost everyone paid me.

My lesson? **Until you value yourself, you can't expect anyone else to do so. Declare what you're worth.**

It's now time for you to recognize your worthiness and acknowledge your magnificence. This is the first step to fully revealing your financial treasures.

Your Financial Treasure #1: Inspiration

Wealth originally meant "well-being"—and there's no doubt that all of us would love to be whole and well with our being. Indeed, almost everyone I've met would love to be wealthy, and even those who are already well-to-do usually desire more affluence.

Know that an abundance of wealth resides in you, ready to materialize. And know that you have a great service to offer the world—every single person does. When you bring that service to your fellow beings, the reward soon follows. This was another important lesson I learned from my early days as a speaker: Your inspiration—that which aligns with your highest values and aspirations—will lead you to your greatest sources of wealth.

Don't minimize yourself by thinking that you don't have inspiration, you can't bring it out, or you don't deserve rich rewards. *You do, you can, and you deserve a vast fortune for your unique contribution to the world.*

Think for a moment about Bill Gates, someone who clearly illustrates the most powerful way I know to create a fortune: *Identify a huge need and fill it.* How many people have used or at least have heard of Microsoft Windows? Billions. What Gates created affects how billions of people work and play. Granted, he's deployed a complex business strategy for amassing his money, but initially, it grew from a germ of an idea—from his inspiration.

Another effective approach is to focus on serving fewer people with a product or service of a high-dollar value. Essentially, these are the two practical approaches to generating large sums of money: Either serve lots of people with something that carries a moderate price tag, or serve a smaller market with a higher-ticket item. Notice that in either case, it's about service—something that inspires you to serve.

It is wise to put the centripetal and the centrifugal forces together. The latter is the force that generates from the inside; it's your personal "axis," the center of you moving outward to serve others. What would you love to bring to the world? *Centripetal* means the force that moves from the outer periphery in toward you—the center. What would those whom you'd love to serve desire to receive? What do they want?

The key questions for you to ask yourself are: *What is my cause? What is my contribution? What would I love to offer to humanity?* and *What does the world need, want, or desire?* I believe that finding something original deep down inside of you is worth any amount of money you'd love to have, but you must draw it out by asking both, *What would I love to give?* and *What do people need?* I wonder what would happen if you were to ask yourself those questions and not stop until you came up with an answer that was worth a billion dollars . . . want to find out? Dig deep! Explore until you've found something you know you can contribute that people truly need or want.

Meanwhile, start to affirm yourself with: *I am a multimillionaire money magnet! Everything I touch turns to gold. I deserve the abundance and wealth that surround me.* Use the Words of Power at the end of this chapter to transform your automatic thinking about how you relate to money.

At the same time, live every day in a humbled state, asking your inner voice and vision to guide you to ever-greater causes and services. Watch your inspiration as it creates a higher appreciation of money, an improved evaluation of yourself, and an abundance of money flowing in your life.

Your Financial Treasure #2: The Wealth You Already Have

If you've completed the exercise in the previous chapter, then you know what your values are and what ranks the highest. You need to look no further in order to find your greatest cache of wealth—it's manifested in your highest value.

This means that you pour your resources into what's most important to you; and not only do you honor this value with your time, attention, and intention, but you also honor it with your money. In this way, the value flourishes in your life—you experience richness in whatever value is highest for you.

In what area of your life do you experience abundance, luxury, and richness? Is it in your health, your spiritual life, your intellect, or in your relationships with family members or friends? If you earnestly consider it, where in your life do you already experience great riches?

The amazing wealth you already have—whatever form it may take, including cash—is the direct result of your values.

Remember, you don't have to choose between financial treasures and what's most important to you. The idea, for example, that you can't be spiritually rich *and* financially prosperous rests on an illusion that spirit and matter are separate—a misperception that I've attempted to put to rest both in the previous chapter and in my book *How to Make One Hell of a Profit and Still Get to Heaven.*

In fact, unless you highly value solvency or cash itself, you'll automatically convert all of your money into whatever is more valuable to you. For example, if your children ranked highest on your values list, that's where your money would go: shelter, food, clothing, education, and experiences for your kids. Likewise, if your business topped the list, you'd no doubt buy equipment, take professional courses, subscribe to trade magazines, and so on—all in order to grow your business.

Here's an important caveat: If you don't put a relatively high value on ready money or some other form of positive cash flow, then you can quickly and easily purchase your way into debt—a subject I'll address shortly.

Let's face it: You're wise to value affluence in the society in which we live. I'm not encouraging you to become infatuated with money and financial wealth and become so greedy that you won't do anything other than hoard it. Yet this one principle—*your values determine your financial well-being*—tells you the difference between those who are wealthy in a conventional sense (meaning they have plenty of money for the lifestyle they've chosen, plus have accumulated enough in savings or investments to feel a sense of security) and those who aren't. It isn't how much money they make, but instead, it's how they manage it. And management is all about one thing: values, which determine your priorities for spending, saving, and investing.

There are people who make less than $30,000 a year who save, invest, and wind up as millionaires; and there are people who make $30,000 *an hour* who go bankrupt. The bottom line is that you can learn all the principles of money management, but **until you value what you've already got and place importance on the accumulation of financial wealth, money will be a fleeting presence in your life.**

Your Financial Treasure #3: Flexibility

One gentleman who'd hired me to consult with him was generating $6.29 million per year, which most people would agree is a great income. He'd called me in because at the end of the year, he was borrowing $327,000 in order to pay his debts to the government for taxes. You might think, *How could a guy pulling more than $6 million a year rack up $327,000 in debt?* But you already know the answer: His values dictated his cash management. Highest on his list were fancy cars, exquisite clothes, world-class travel, rare art, and front-row seating for entertainment—you get the idea. He had a low value on paying his taxes and saving money. So he'd accumulated plenty of nice things, but he had nothing left come tax time.

On the other side, his secretary was earning $24,000 a year and saving $400 a month. Her taxes were withheld from her paycheck, so the $400 in savings went straight to her own net worth's bottom line. By the time I met the two of them, she was far closer to financial independence than he was.

Appreciate—or depreciate!

Unless you appreciate the money that comes to you—which is another way of saying that you value it and are grateful for it—it's not going to be part of your life for long. Whatever you don't appreciate will depreciate!

Money automatically flows to those who appreciate it the most. It automatically finds its way to those who study and practice the principles of wise money management. People who devalue money—who say it's unimportant or even "evil"—tend to spend their lives working for it. Those who value money—who save it and use it to enhance the world around them—end up with money working for them. Know that if you have to work for money, you're its slave, yet you're its master when you put it to work for you.

Let's be really clear about this. I know I'm repeating myself, but it bears saying again: **Financial independence and having money have nothing to do with how much money you make. They have everything to do with how you manage the money that comes your way. And how you manage money has everything to do with your hierarchy of values.**

If you've discovered that a lack of appreciation for money may be holding you back from having the cash flow you'd love, there's good news: You don't have to perpetuate this illusion of scarcity. You can alter your perceptions and even change your values.

As you already know, you have your own unique, ordered set of values. If building wealth didn't even show up on your list or it appeared somewhere long after the top ten, then there's a simple exercise you can do to boost its rankings.

Link it to what you love.

Make a list of reasons why saving money and building wealth could change your life and how it could contribute to the people you care about and love. Don't just write down one or two benefits. List more than 100 (and if you're ready to go for it, list 200 or even 300 or more) reasons why saving money and building wealth will serve you and those you love. Get family members involved if you think it would be wise and help reinforce the new ideas and feelings you're generating about wealth. Likewise, while you're making this giant list, be sure to fully engage. Get inspired, be thoughtful, and entertain yourself with the possibilities.

Next, focus on what you ranked as your highest value when you completed the discovering-your-values exercise in the previous chapter. How will saving money and building wealth help you experience richness in this area to an even greater degree? Once again, come up with at least 100 ways in which money supports your highest value. Now take a look at your second highest value and so on, continuing down the list. By the time you're done, you'll have hundreds of reasons why saving money and building wealth can make a significant contribution to your life—and the lives of people you love.

If you link saving and investing money to whatever is already most important to you, you won't subtract from your wealth, you'll naturally add to it! Remember how you automatically convert your cash into your values? When saving is tightly connected with your highest values—whether children, philanthropy, social action, business, or whatever those values are—your cash will be converted to savings in support of those values *if you've realized enough reasons for it.*

In this exercise, you're priming yourself for a new cash-management strategy, one that includes appreciation for what saving and building wealth can bring to the rest of your life. When you've completed this exercise, you're ready to implement some of the key strategies for accumulating the material riches you'd love to have.

Your Financial Treasure #4: Cash Flow

Whether you have a lot or a little—a flood or a trickle—money is no doubt flowing in your life. As you just read, that flow is directed by your values. And if it's important to you to keep some of the money you earn (that is, to save it and invest it for your future and the future of what you believe in), then certain principles make all the difference.

Pay yourself first.

People who pay themselves first get ahead, and people who pay themselves last fall behind. The former become more wealthy, and the latter become poorer. It's as simple as that. Really.

What does it mean to pay yourself first? It means that you prioritize your saving plan above every other expense. That's right: *You* come before the electric bill, the mortgage, and even before taxes. This doesn't mean that you're not going to pay for those things anymore—it's just that *you* get paid first. Period.

Life isn't only about serving other people. You must figure out how to reward yourself in the process—not with trinkets such as furniture, snack food, or a new car, but with accumulating, escalating savings, and then investments. This isn't about earning money so that you can pay other people for services and stuff—it's about keeping some for yourself, too.

Most people who get in the habit of paying everyone else first usually do so just because that's what everyone else seems to do. Yet if you've already heard about the principle of paying yourself first and have even accepted that it's wise in theory but you're still not practicing it, I may be able to offer some insight.

Some people say, "When I get extra money, that's when I'll start saving. I have too many bills to start a savings plan right now." That means they're valuing everything and everyone above themselves! Again, this is an issue of values, not income.

Similarly, if you don't do what you love or love what you do, your self-worth automatically lowers. (To address this issue, see Chapter 5, "Power: Your Vocational Treasures.") When you lower your self-worth, it becomes more difficult to pay yourself for your actions or services—you feel less worthy to receive. And this can be a self-perpetuating cycle, as those who give themselves more . . . usually receive more, and those who give themselves less . . . usually receive less. To those who have, more is given; to those who have not, more is taken away. According to the ancient proverb and also the modern scientific principle of "preferential attachment," the rich get richer and the poor get poorer.

When you think you don't have enough to pay yourself and you have a finite poverty consciousness, you act in a financially self-depreciating way. Those who believe themselves to be worth the investment, however, begin to unfold ever-greater lives that attract other people's investments. Until you invest in your own inspirations—by earning money from doing what you love and then paying yourself first out of that income—nobody else will. Yet people will invest in the certainty of the soul or in people who have great and true worth. They'll invest in inspirations and services done with enthusiasm, love, and gratitude—those done with spirit. In practical terms, this means that an employer will reward a worker who performs a job with inspiration, and customers will reward a business that delivers a product or service with inspiration.

Every time you receive an inspiring idea from your soul in the form of a message, calling, or vision, *pay yourself*. Reward yourself for listening and acting in wisdom.

Start FAST: Turn your piggy banks into biggie banks.

It was my own experience with forgetting to start saving for my income taxes one year that caused me to refine what I call the FAST system: "forced automatic savings technique."

Because I'm in business for myself, I don't have my taxes withheld from a paycheck so that means I pay Uncle Sam (also known as the Internal Revenue Service) out of my own bank account. When I first started saving—which, incidentally, was only $10 a day, $50 a week, $200 a month—that was a lot for me, even on a chiropractor's salary, because I had bills and debts. I had plenty of excuses about why I couldn't save. But I started with $200 a month because, even though it would be a stretch, I thought I could do it.

So I set up an automatic-withdrawal plan with my bank: Every month, $200 disappeared from my business account and went straight to a personal-savings account that I didn't touch. What's more, I didn't get to think about it, second-guess the transaction, or make up reasons why I should put it off until next month—it just happened automatically.

A few months went by and I found I wasn't missing the money—and I was saving $200 a month! So I bumped it up to $300. Then another few months went by, and again I thought, *I don't even notice that I don't have that money to spend! It's not interfering with my lifestyle. Somehow, my business is expanding to give me the money I need.* (Ever notice how that works? If you have "extra" cash, you always find somewhere to spend it, and if you're short, you always find some way to stretch your dollar or come up with the money to pay for things you really need.) That's why "forced" savings makes sense: It forces you to either earn more or cut spending so that your priority—saving—is always intact.

I remember when I broke the $1,000 mark for saving each month. That was a big day for me! I was starting to see the light at the end of the tunnel and feeling as if financial independence might be mine someday. It could be 50 years, but I was on my way.

Then I realized that I hadn't paid my taxes yet, and I hadn't been setting aside money for it either, so it meant that I had to go to my savings account and move cash to cover my taxes. There went my savings—straight to the government. Boy, did that make me mad! But I learned my lesson: For entrepreneurs especially, a FAST program has to include money set aside for taxes, too. I started matching the amount I put into savings with the appropriate percentage I was to put into a special tax account. That way, I could still pay myself first but the government came second, because I knew that if I didn't pay them, I could interfere with and diminish what I'd saved for myself.

Those are the FAST priorities: Pay yourself, pay the taxes, and everyone else comes after.

At the end of that next year, I was loving how it was working for me: FAST was the perfect acronym. My savings were in order, my taxes were paid, and my business was growing to meet my new plan. I ended that year saving $1,700 a month. About every three months thereafter, I've raised my savings 10 percent. (For all this time, on every occasion that I raised my savings, I also raised my tax set-aside.) And with each new quarter, more business opportunities have arrived to cover my plan, and I've watched an acceleration of my wealth and business.

You can do this, too! It doesn't matter how much you start with—*your piggy banks can become biggie banks.* What matters is that you start. Now. Not when you think you have some extra cash, not when you pay off X, Y, or Z, and not when you win the lottery—do it now. Start paying yourself first, FAST.

Save for your immortality.

Immortal wealth is that which lasts beyond your physical life. To save for a rainy day can be like putting drops in a bucket, but to save for immortality can be like reaching for the heavens. For many people, the act of saving for future generations is more inspiring than a less ambitious plan. Eternal investments certainly have greater returns than short-term ones.

Think and feel right now about what causes you'd love to invest in, what immortal dreams you'd love to leave as your legacy, and something that would inspire you to immortal action. Imagine what investments you feel called to dedicate your savings to, and realize that you can't give without receiving. **The greater cause you give to, the greater cause you become.** As you invest in ever-greater causes, so too will others invest with ever-greater ease in your immortal dreams.

Consider opening an "immortal savings account," where you deposit a portion of your savings each month and earmark it for your legacy.

When you spend more, save more.

Here's an important lesson I learned from disciplining myself with FAST: Every time I wanted to raise my lifestyle, I raised my savings and taxes accounts an equal amount. That was my check-and-balance system. If I wasn't willing to do that, then I wasn't ready to raise my lifestyle. (If I didn't have an extra $700 to deposit into my savings and taxes accounts each month, for example, then it didn't make sense to spend $700 a month on, say, a new Prius.)

Before I had been buying new things and making new financial commitments without raising my savings and tax account payments, and then I'd accumulate debt or depreciating items. Let me put this plainly: Debt doesn't raise your self-worth, and this can interfere with any efforts to build wealth. When your tastes outweigh your finances, you weigh yourself down. When your consumption outdoes your production, you beat yourself down.

Credit-card companies know that the majority of individuals attempt to pay off their debts eventually, so they lend money to most people because of these probabilities. There's nothing inherently wrong with credit cards, but the careless use of them can lead to substantial debt. To spend beyond what you have is usually unwise unless a return on the expenditure is almost guaranteed. Paying interest instead of making interest isn't usually wise, either. If you get behind with your creditors, your interest payments can mount rapidly. But if you save first and allow the savings interest to grow, purchasing with cash can make quite a difference to your financial well-being. No escalating debt means greater acceleration of savings.

Paying with cash can often help you prioritize what you buy—its tangible form helps you keep in mind what's more and less important to you. It's a sign of wisdom to make purchases consciously instead of impulsively and without thought to the impact on your overall money situation.

Consider carrying enough money with you so that you don't ever feel a sense of lack. Like a gas tank that's almost empty, which makes you feel less secure, a nearly empty pocket can also make you feel less financially secure. Carry with you as much as you'd love to make in a day.

Give anonymously.

The experience of growing wealth may manifest gratitude quite naturally. You might feel compelled to give something back by contributing money to some worthy person, cause, place of worship, or to any source of inspiration. As you make your decisions about giving, you're wise to consider this: When you give to someone and they know you're the giver, you also give them reason to thank you—"the part." But when you give anonymously, you give them the opportunity to thank "the whole"—the universe or its origin. Imagine how much more profound an experience it is for the recipient to feel gratitude to the immortal whole rather than thankful for the mortal part.

What's more, when you allow others to become infatuated with you for your giving, you also encourage them to become resentful. At first gifts are appreciated, and then they're expected; and if you don't continue to give, eventually a depreciating cycle of infatuation and resentment can start. Through anonymous giving, however, you encourage gratitude for the universe. To the degree that you induce gratitude to the universe in others, you receive the gifts of inner peace, inner power, and secrecy.

Your Financial Treasure #5: Mastery

Once you start to force your savings to accelerate, manage your spending so as not to create unwieldy debt, and give anonymously, mastery of money begins! Now you're setting up a strategy that builds great fortunes. I've been amazed at what has resulted from my early efforts—monetary growth by regular increments into big savings and big contributions. Once you commit to a savings plan and to giving back, it's as if the universe starts to bring you new ways to be sure you keep it going.

When you have $100, you get $100 opportunities; with $1,000 saved, you get $1,000 opportunities. With $1 million saved—you guessed it—you get million-dollar opportunities. Imagine what types of opportunities billionaire Bill Gates receives every day!

Are you getting my message? There's a profound benefit to saving and managing your money wisely. Every time you save, you not only get the benefit of building a nest egg and compound interest, but you attract new associations in your life, new ideas, and new opportunities. There's a geometric compounding that opens the doorway for even greater wealth.

When you save money and manage it wisely, you begin feeling more entrepreneurial. You start receiving opportunities and ideas, and you come into contact with people who think along the same lines, producing brilliant business ideas. You have more courage to "do your own thing," and you have even greater impetus to do what you love, love what you do, and follow all of your inspirations. That's mastery.

When I first started my FAST program, I was frightened. Even though the income from my practice was comfortable by most people's standards, I was scared to start putting some of it aside for me. But I did it anyway, and I'm encouraging you to do the same if you haven't already. This is the road to financial mastery, and you have the power within you right now to take this first step—then you can take the next one and the next one. Push yourself like someone who's just learning how to run. You start out slow, worried about getting sore—maybe even feeling the limits of your muscles and lungs. Yet as you continue to push yourself, you also feel those "limits" expanding. You find your stride, stop worrying, and simply start becoming inspired by fully exercising what Grand Organized Design has provided you with. Not only are you motivated to keep going and keep getting stronger, but you begin to see how your intention and creativity have put you in this place of awe and wonder.

Words of Power

I spend and save money wisely, and I am prosperous.

I save for my soul's grand purpose, and
I have immortal wealth.

I value my time and space, and I am wealthy.

I pay myself first because I love myself.

I am generous, and the more I give, the more I receive.

I am open to receiving abundance.

I have the wisdom to be paid for whatever I love doing.

→ CHAPTER FIVE ←

Power: Your Vocational Treasures

"Knowledge of the great truths only appears in action and labor."
— Albert Schweitzer

When someone interviews for a job with me, they're in for an unusual conversation. Once we've established that the appropriate skills, talent, and drive are all present in the individual applying for the position, I whip out my bankbook, pen a check for $5 million, and inquire, "Exactly how do I spell your name?"

As soon as I've written the person's name in the "Pay to the Order of" line, I ask, "If I gave you this check for $5 million right now, what would you do with your life?" The answer provides tremendous insight into what this person's true vocation is—and whether that fits in with the job I have to offer.

In fact, if the answer doesn't resemble a description of the position for which they're applying, I let them know that I won't be hiring them and prepare myself to interview the next candidate. Their truthful response has told me they're not a match for our company, and I need to look for other candidates who love what they do so much that $5 million fuels their inspiration to fulfill the career position I'm offering instead of taking them off in a completely different direction.

Once when interviewing a man in his 50s who had a warm smile and a stylish briefcase, I wrote the check and asked him my stock question: "If I gave you this check for $5 million right now, what would you do with your life?"

We'd been having a favorable interview so far: He'd spoken enthusiastically about what he wanted to do for and with the company, and up to this point, it seemed that he'd be a good match for the managerial position. But then his eyes got a faraway look, and he started talking about how much he loved woodworking: the smell of fresh-cut pine, cedar, cherry, and walnut; the feel of finely sanded lumber; the transformation of rough wood into precise shapes; and the challenge of crafting beautiful details.

While he was in this reverie, I gently interrupted him. "You obviously love woodworking. Why don't you pursue that?"

He probably thought I was kidding because he laughed.

"Seriously," I said. "If you're such a great manager and would love to be a woodworker and furniture maker, yet you haven't figured out how to manage your own life so that you can do what you love, why would I expect you to successfully manage my company?"

He began to waver when he realized I wasn't joking. "Well, John," he said as he tried to convince me, "I'd really love to come work for you. . . ."

I didn't hire him, and he left my office with something to think about.

A few weeks later, he returned to my office offering his personal thanks and letting me know that he'd begun to pursue his dream. After our conversation, he'd realized that he possessed the skills to run his own company yet hadn't followed through on it because owning a furniture-making shop hadn't fit into his idea of a "respectable career." He was over that now, though, and was feeling incredibly grateful for the push I'd given him. He sent several elegant wood pieces to my office to express his appreciation.

When hiring, you're not doing anyone a disservice by passing over uninspired employees. And as an employee, you're not doing anyone any favors by clinging to a job or company that doesn't help awaken you to your own magnificence. Instead, whether employer or employee, seek to match work and worker. The motto behind this is: **Love what you do and do what you love.**

How can you make that happen for yourself and for those who work with you? Dig deep to mine the vocational treasures of calling, clarity, and congruence.

Your Vocational Treasure #1: Calling

Work can be a drudge or a dream—or anything in between. Like everything else in your life, you determine exactly what it's going to be.

If you're waking up each morning on fire, feeling called to great service and devoted to an inspiring purpose, vision, and mission, no doubt you feel as if work isn't work at all: It's a kind of play with monetary benefits. On the other hand, if you turn back the covers each morning and groan, "Oh man, I wish I could just stay in bed," and dread your 9-to-5 (or whatever hours you keep) work, then surely you feel as if your job is a "burden" and a "necessary evil."

On the continuum of "job satisfaction" that employers are always trying to measure and employees are always hoping to max out, there's a level at which some people feel a mystical draw to serve in a particular way. They feel that this is what they were meant to do, and this particular profession is their *raison d'être*—their purpose here on Earth. These people still have all kinds of ups and downs in their work: They perceive "successes" and "failures," feel "happy" and "sad," experience "contentment" and "frustration," and so on—just like everyone else. Having a job you love doesn't exempt you from the human experience, of course. The difference is that those who are called to their work feel a kind of "fit" to their profession; it's what Buddhists call "right livelihood"—making a living in such a way that benefits both oneself and others.

If you're not having this kind of experience yet and would love to, it's time to get in touch with your true vocation . . . your *calling.*

The 1996 book by James Hillman, *The Soul's Code: In Search of Character and Calling,* puts forth a theory that you simply need to pay attention to your young life in order to spot early rumblings of your calling, even if it wasn't in full voice yet. He recounts how both famous people and average folk experience the call. For example, actress and singer Judy Garland received her first accolades for an impromptu performance at two years old. She had watched another young girl's solo and had been transfixed by the sight of it. According to her sister's account, Judy (born Frances Gumm) turned to her father then and pleaded, "Can I do that, Daddy?" He encouraged her, and the next chance she had, the toddler stepped onstage and belted out her version of "Jingle Bells," to which the crowd roared in approval. She started singing again, louder this time, and the crowd responded in kind. Eventually, her father had to pull her off stage. Hillman observes: "Garland of the Hollywood Bowl and Carnegie Hall was already there in two-year-old Baby Gumm."

That's a pretty dramatic, clear-cut example. But a sense of calling isn't limited to those who hear it strongly right from the start. Sometimes you have to look for subtler clues: The child who referred to pill bugs, lizards, cats, and dogs she'd collected as "my little friends" might be called to veterinary medicine; the one who lost herself in books might find her vocation in writing, and so on.

Your calling can be amplified by applying some time and attention to it. If you're not already feeling "called" to your profession, you can look at other areas of your life, both at the present time and in the past, when you've felt uplifted and inspired in some way by something.

But what if after looking back and looking around you, you don't see a pattern yet? What if you can't identify the times in your past when you felt as if you were in your element, doing what you were meant to do? Here's help.

Show yourself the money.

You might start with my interview question: If I were to give *you* $5 million right now, what would you do with your life? Be honest. What makes your heart beat faster? What brings a tear to your eye?

Ultimately, this exercise is about being true to yourself. A business is like a body: It gives you signs and symptoms to help guide you to your truth. If your current position, profession, or line of business feels "dysfunctional" or "diseased," take this as a clear signal that it's time to reconnect with the truth of who you really are. What a treasure it is to be able to read those signs and symptoms and take action! Just as in your physical body, your business, your relationships, your social network—anywhere you engage with the world—gives you feedback to be true to yourself. The universe operates as a matrix, trying to lead every one of us back to authenticity and love.

Ask, ask, and ask again.

Tonight, get down on your knees beside your bed like a child and humble yourself before the universe. Create a version of the following statement that fits your spiritual beliefs, and say, "Dear Universe! Dear God! Dear Source! Dear Soul! Reveal to me what I'm here to do." Be quiet and listen. If your answers aren't made known to you tonight, get down on your knees again tomorrow night and every night thereafter until you hear your calling loud and clear. Even if you have an idea about your calling or feel as if you're absolutely clear about why you're here, this remains a powerful exercise in humbling yourself to the ordering field. If you're sincerely humble, the chatter of the many voices in your mind turn into The Voice. You hear your calling. And when the voice and vision on the inside are greater than all opposition and opinion on the outside, you open the treasure chest containing all your vocational riches.

Make a declaration.

As you begin to hear the inner voice that reveals your next steps of purpose, make note. Write a first draft, and then refine it as you grow more connected and committed to your purpose, giving it a new dimension and crafting statements that reflect your inspiration to this great calling.

Here's a format for making this important declaration:

> *"I,* [your name], *hereby declare before myself and others that my primary purpose in life is to be . . . by doing . . . so I may have . . ."*

Fill in the blanks, and then sign and date it. Once you've written your purpose, you've taken a powerful step toward living it, loving what you do, and doing what you love.

Your Vocational Treasure #2: Clarity

Figuring out what you love and, thus, what your calling may be certainly gives you a delicious taste of clarity. Getting entirely clear in your vocation, though, means deciding what you'd love to do—and where you'd love to take yourself, your business, and/or your career. The idea is to determine what you'd love to do for free—and then figure out how you can be handsomely rewarded for it. It's another one of those dichotomies: What's the thing you'll share for nothing, and what are the steps necessary to put you in a position to gratefully receive everything?

Whether you've just started on the path you'd most love to travel, are a long way down the road, or even if your ideal professional track is still just an idea, you can take it to the next level by gaining greater clarity. In business, clarity equals vitality.

For nearly 25 years, I've said: "The universe is my playground! The world is my home! Every country is another room in my house, and every city is another platform to share my heart-inspiring message! I'll do whatever it takes, travel whatever distance, and pay whatever price to offer my services of love. I'll set foot in every country on the face of the earth until this aspect of my mission is fulfilled!" That's how I put my vision into words, expressing what I imagine for myself in my professional pursuits, and I reiterate that statement to myself and to the universe every single day of my life. I'm called to be a student and a teacher of universal principles, and my vision is to enact that all over the world.

Sometimes people tell me that they don't have time to clarify "all this stuff." People who work for someone else say they already devote too many hours doing a job that stresses them out, and entrepreneurs say they're so busy responding to customers and employees that they just can't justify taking the "time off" to think about and design their businesses.

What are the excuses you use to avoid examining the difference between where you are and where you would love to be? Everyone has "perfectly good reasons," yet time spent on getting a detailed picture, plan, and purpose for where you're headed can *save* you hours of work: You can earn more money in less time. So the saying goes: Working *on* your business pays more dividends than working *in* your business. In other words, whatever time or money you devote to detailing your vision and mission—and the plan that supports them—gets paid back to you in both efficiency and effectiveness. If you own the business, your efforts will usually lead to greater profits, improved employee retention, and an increasing return on your investments. If you work for someone else, your labors will usually lead to opportunities for growth in your profession, whether that means you'll rise within the company, move on to another, or start your own.

Many people also get that glazed-over, glassy-eyed look whenever anyone starts talking about mission and vision. They either think it's "fluffy" and not really important to business, or else they're just cynical; they've heard it all before, and how has it really helped them? Again, think about the excuses you've come up with in the past—did they result from you being jaded about the whole concept?

Skepticism around these two words *mission* and *vision* is pretty thick, and I acknowledge that it's hard to cut through that disbelief until you actually experience the effects of clarifying your own mission and vision and putting them to work in your own life. I remember one fellow who visited me in my office, a divorce lawyer who was leaving his profession and going into the field of conflict resolution. He was obviously onto something: He felt as if his time as an attorney had served him well, he knew what didn't work, and he felt called to help people end relationships with a greater sense of fulfillment. (Eventually, he wrote a book about resolving marriages without massive devastation.)

He asked me, "How did you get your national and international network off the ground? What did you use and do?"

"It's my vision," I told him.

"Right, I understand that," he said, "but what did you *do,* specifically?"

"I held a clear vision for what I wanted to create," I explained.

"No, no, not that. What brochures did you use? What are your marketing pieces? What was your marketing strategy?"

I pulled out my "Breakthrough to Higher Power, VIP Seminar" brochure—a small thing that listed the event price at $777. I pointed to it and said, "That's all I've got."

"No, no," he insisted. "I'm talking about—" he was getting exasperated. "How did you market this seminar so that people around the world are interested in it now?"

"I. Don't. Have. Anything. Else. This is it. People tell people about it. Meanwhile, I have a clear vision of what I'd love to create, and that vision is bigger than the world."

Obviously frustrated, he replied, "I guess I'm just not communicating what I want here."

No matter what I said or did, I couldn't get through to him, *because he was thinking in terms of tangibles, not intangibles; his thinking level was local, not global.* Had he gotten that and expanded his consciousness, he might have made a worldwide impact, but unless you have a vision *beyond* the local, you won't make a global impact. Expanding your consciousness means that more of your vision manifests; you won't always notice a direct correlation between what you do and what happens, but you will notice that some of what you do has a bigger and broader outreach because your consciousness is expanded.

Just as plants grow toward the source of light, people grow toward enlightenment. When you enlighten yourself by acknowledging your magnificence—following your calling and creating clarity about your mission and vision—other people are also drawn to you. They want to align with you and see you shine. They invest in you and your ideas, buy your products and services, and advance you through the corporate ranks.

Skillful marketing can add to that kind of attraction, but the most significant part of the recipe is your vision, which needs to extend beyond the sphere that you'd love to impact. You can't make a difference in the world and have something felt all over the planet until you have an astronomical vision. You must stand out beyond your goal and see the earth instead of standing on it looking out; your horizon and perspective must be bigger. Once your perspective comes from a different horizon, the impact of your product, service, or idea fills that domain. Your consciousness is out in that realm—therefore, it resonates there.

A chiropractor in one of the larger U.S. cities came to my seminar where I spoke about this principle, and he had a local practice that drew people from about a ten-mile radius. When he heard me say this—*you can't make a difference in your city, state, nation, or world unless you have a vision that comes from the sphere beyond it*—he really got it. He immediately started to affirm to himself that his healing center was a beacon of light to the world. He repeated that exact phrase, *My center is a beacon of light to the world,* as words of power in order to expand his consciousness.

On my advice, he also bought a globe, marked his office on it, and fixed in his mind where his practice was in relation to the rest of the world. Every day he'd look at it, spin it, and imagine that people were coming to see him from around the globe. And within a matter of weeks, people did come to him from different states, and soon thereafter from Asia, and then from other parts of the world—just because he opened up his receptivity and put his consciousness beyond the domain in which he knew he'd love to impact.

What would you love to do? How would you love to serve? Where do you see yourself headed? How far and wide do you envision your impact? With a clear vision, you can put the soul back into the corporate body, whether you own the corporation or are a part of it. At last, you can stop looking for something else to make it "better." How many times have you said to yourself, *Once I get that promotion, I'll like my job and feel fulfilled?* Infuse your working life with spirit and you'll start climbing from any plateau, or—like my woodworking friend—you'll finally take the necessary steps to get that business off the ground.

When you're clear on your mission and vision, you'll also have a message. That message will filter down to the people who work for you and the clients or customers who use your service. They'll know who you are, how that serves them, and even how it serves you. You create a kind of transparency of self—an added dimension of clarity—that's very attractive to others. This holds true in every kind of business: Even if you're selling widgets online and you're providing products to people you'll never meet, communicate a clear mission and message to every single buyer.

Do this now.

Dig down inside yourself right now, and pull out of your heart and soul what's truly most important to you and what you'd truly be inspired to be, do, and have for you and your organization. (If you haven't done so already, go back and "make a declaration," as described earlier in the chapter.) Now consider all the talents you've acquired through your years of working and correlate them with all the potential needs of those you serve: customers, clients, supervisors, colleagues, and coworkers. Start with what you're certain about, and build around this until you feel sure that you know what you and your organization are dedicated to offering in the way of service.

Don't lie to yourself, saying that you don't know. Look at what your life's journey has led you toward. Your most prominent skills have emerged all around your chief aim and its direction. This is what you'd love to do; it's your service. And what you'd love to have—that is, the results of your service—describes your reward. By pursuing your life's true path, you'll also shape your business or organization toward what you love. Listen to your inner self, as it will continue to guide you in this endeavor, helping you constantly evolve and grow.

If you align your goals with a company's or an organization's objectives, your rate of achievement can grow as long as you allow yourself to shine and emerge. The key is to develop a plan. Start with what is last and work your way back to what is first, breaking down the dream and mission into ever-smaller actions and details until there's no procrastination, hesitation, or even frustration. By the inch it is a cinch! Planning your dreams can be inspiring and can offer creative new ways to fulfill what's most important for you and those you serve.

Pay attention to what works.

Defining and refining your plan requires that you notice what works—and keep doing it until you find something greater. Something that I learned from a great teacher, Ira Hayes, is to keep and update a checklist of everything that you've proven to work in your life. I call mine the "Did I do it?" list, and it amounts to a self-accountability system for those activities that I know work for me. This is a simple process you can start today without much effort at all. Tuck a notebook in your pocket or create a new file on your computer—just figure out an easy way for you to record the items.

My list has about 30 activities on it that I know, if I do them every single day, will result in the rest of my life unfolding at its greatest. Once you have your checklist, reflect on it in the morning before you start the day, and then look at it again in the evening to check off everything that you've done. It's a no-brainer that will keep you focused on what you think is most fulfilling to you.

Your Vocational Treasure #3: Congruence

"I want to be successful."

The doctor had approached me, asking if he could hire me as a consultant to help with his practice. When I asked what he'd love to achieve, he'd said that the practice wasn't as big as he wanted it to be, and he thought that I was the man to turn things around. But there were a few more things I needed to hear from him first.

"Great!" I began. "Where are you already successful?"

"I don't think you heard me. I *want* to be successful. That's what I need you for."

"Oh, I did hear you," I assured him. "Where are you already successful in your life?"

"But I'm not!" he insisted.

With equal intensity, I responded, "Yes, you are! Look and then look again. You already have success"—and now that you've come this far in this book, you can guess what I said next—*"according to the hierarchy of your values*. Look carefully this time. In what area of life are you already experiencing your success?"

Now he was starting to get it: **Success isn't limited to the arena of professional achievements.**

"My marriage is pretty amazing. My wife and I have a wonderful relationship, we've been married for ten years, and we still love each other—that's success, I suppose."

"And where else are you successful?" I asked.

His eyes brightened. "My son and I have a great relationship, too. I'm his baseball coach, and our team may win the pennant this year. We have a terrific time together, and he's doing really well. We're close both on the field and at home."

"Where else—" I didn't even finish before he continued.

"My mother-in-law! She lives with us, and we love it. All of us get along well, and it's so rewarding to watch my son developing such a strong bond with his grandmother. Our family has its ups and downs, but we can love each other through anything. Most people can't say that, can they? And I'm a lay leader at my church—sometimes I do classes for people and get great feedback. Those are successes, too."

I encouraged him and replied, "Can you see, then, that you've had successes in your life?"

He nodded and continued, "My lawn and garden are thriving, too. We make that a family project, and it's one of the things we're all proud to have accomplished together. That's another kind of success, right?"

"Absolutely," I said. "Now let me explain something: For you to feel as if you're a 'failure'—that is, not as successful as you'd love to be—you must be comparing your achievements to someone else. Who do you compare yourself to and find yourself 'lacking' in some way?"

"I guess I'm comparing myself to this doctor who lives up on top of the hill. He's got a big house, expensive cars . . ."

"All right," I agreed, "those can be nice things. But I have a question: How's his relationship with his wife?"

"Soon to be divorced for the second time," he reported.

"What about kids?"

"It's kind of rough: One son is into drugs, and they're having behavioral problems with the younger one."

"Okay, what about the yard?"

"It's fine, I guess. The grass gets cut regularly and nothing's overgrown. They pay a gardener to maintain it for them—I'm not sure they even know it's out there."

"And the in-laws?"

"At this point, I think he'd do anything to stay away from both sets of them—he doesn't get along with any of them. I don't think they're on speaking terms now."

I asked, "Can you see that this man has one kind of success, according to the hierarchy of his values, and you have a completely different set of values and therefore different areas of success in your life?"

He nodded. "Now that you point it out, yes."

"And would you sacrifice your form of success to have his?" I asked.

Now he was shaking his head. "No way."

As we continued our conversation, I counseled this doctor to realize that the level of success he was experiencing in his practice and in his life were a direct result of his values. It's unwise to minimize your form of success, I told him, thinking that someone else's is greater. That's not to say that you can't expand your success in any area or embrace the kind of success you see others experiencing right now—it's just that you don't want to limit your notions of success, minimize yourself, or subordinate yourself to other people. It's all determined by your hierarchy of values.

By the end of our conversation, this gentleman was in a completely different state of mind, and I could see him holding back tears. "I really would rather have what I already have than anything else. My family, my home, my church . . . I wouldn't trade them for anything." He smiled at me and then asked, "But is there some way you can help me grow my practice, too?"

Of course there was. And this was the greatest starting point: An awareness of true gratitude for what he already had—for the successes he was already experiencing. Now he was ready to stop beating himself up and start honoring his success. And here's the real treasure he found: When you're grateful for what you already have, you receive or experience even more to be grateful for!

Similarly, when I was hired to consult with a large high-tech firm based in Houston, I discovered that about 75 percent of the people working there were uninspired by what they were doing. My job, as I saw it, wasn't to "motivate" everyone to love their jobs, but instead to help them figure out what *would* inspire them. By the time I was done there, some decided that they needed to leave the company, and the rest decided to get focused—and after this shift, the company grew.

Keep in mind that those who left weren't "failures," nor was the company they left a "failure." These individuals got clear about where they really wanted to go, and it just so happened to be out the door. *They got in touch with their values, and they saw that it was time to focus on something else.* Inspiration doesn't always lead you to stay put; in fact, it often moves you to something greater. Not tapping into your inspiration is what creates "dead weight," "baggage," and "overhead"—something no employer seeks to increase in his or her organization. The most vital ventures are powered by people who love what they do.

The following are exercises you can do for yourself or give to employees, just as I did at IBM. They'll help you make your work life congruent with what's most important to you.

Empty the junk drawer of your mind.

I call this "distraction resolution." It helps you stay focused on what's important while heightening your congruency between activities and values, as well as goals. Here's how you do it:

- Make a list of every single thing that's taking up space and time in your mind, whether it's personal, business, physical, or financial; anything you did and feel guilty about;

or something you need to do a day, week, month, or year from now. Jot down anything that's distracting you from being present in the here and now. Follow your stream of consciousness and clear it out of your mind by writing it down.

- Once you're done—not while you're writing, but after you've spent about ten minutes getting it all out—look at the list you've created and see if there's anything in there that's junk. Ask yourself, *Is there anything here that I can't do anything about? Is there anything in my head that I can just get rid of?*

- Now consider if there's anyone whom you can delegate the remainder to. Or are you holding yourself back because you haven't been exercising the skill of delegation (whether that's because you're unskilled or you don't think there's anyone who can handle this for you)? You'll be surprised by how many things you're doing that are actually low priority—and that you could be delegating to someone else. Who could do this instead? Put that person's initials next to the item.

- If there are things there for you to do—things that you know would be best done by you, and you know that you can do something about them—write your initials beside them and assign a date for beginning that item. Be realistic, and if it's a long-term project, go ahead and chunk it down into smaller pieces, and decide to delegate or date those pieces for yourself.

The follow-up is simple: Once you've noticed the things that can be dumped, it's easy to just "take them out" of your mind. And if you find yourself thinking about them again, you can remind yourself: *Oh yeah, that was one of those things that I'm not going to do anything about. Next!* Then you can delegate those items you've chosen to, and you can integrate your own tasks and projects into whatever scheduling system you already use. I recommend creating 30 to 60 days' worth of daily to-do forms, assigning each project a fitting time. Then you can *forget* about all those items and focus on what's important to do today.

This is the difference between efficiency and effectiveness: *Efficiency means getting everything done that needs doing in a timely and professional manner, and effectiveness means doing only those things that are important enough to get done.* You can have both if you (1) align your activities, values, and goals; (2) delegate everything that wouldn't wisely be done by you; and (3) dump anything that's just "junk." With this exercise, you identify distractions, dumps, delegations, do's, and dates. You clear your mind and create congruency between your actions and dreams.

Align goals and values.

Start by drawing three columns on a piece of paper, labeling them from left to right: *My Activities, My Dreams,* and *Business Objectives & Mission.*

— **Column 1: My Activities.** Make a list down the left side of the page of everything you do in your day at work, including the things you like, those you dislike, the ones that frustrate or bore you, and everything that's fun or energizing.

— **Column 2: My Dreams.** In the middle column, write down your most important dreams, your five highest demonstrated values, and the vision for your life that you'd most love to fulfill. This helps you compose your personal mission.

— **Column 3: Business Objectives & Mission.** Record the mission and objectives of your company in the third column. If you work for someone else, find out from your direct superior what he or she says are the mission and objectives. If you own the company, write down the clear mission and objectives you've defined for your business.

Between columns 1 and 2, jot down how each of your activities helps you fulfill your dreams, including (and perhaps especially) the ones you'd prefer not to do. Ask yourself, *How is doing this activity helping me fulfill my dreams and do what's most meaningful to me?* At first, with each of those less-than-favorite items, you're probably going to say, "It doesn't!" But look at it again with the idea of creating a new perception about this activity in your mind. Don't give up, and don't give yourself excuses. Keep at it until you can answer the question: *How does this activity help me fulfill my highest values?*

In fact, write down not just one answer, but a minimum of 20 ways in which every activity helps you get what you most love. At first you'll think you can't do it, but I assure you that you can. I've helped entire companies full of people get it done, and during this exercise, links are made between the brain (that perceives whatever it might about those activities) and the heart (that can feel love for those activities). When such links are created by you doing this, suddenly no task is tedious. Once you realize that you're working for yourself—your values, your mission, and your dreams—no matter if you're the boss or an employee, you'll suddenly feel permission to love what you're doing, and you can go out and do what you love with enthusiasm. Wouldn't you love to love going to work every day? This is how you can!

You'll also discover how serving the mission of the company fulfills you when you do this linking process with columns 2 and 3. The job that you're in right now is no mistake. It's a transition, if nothing else, giving you tools, contacts, experience, opportunities, and skills. It's definitely giving you something! When you link your job description to the most meaningful values in your life, then link the mission of the company to that, the very job that may not have inspired you in the past can become wonderfully uplifting. You'll automatically have more energy and vitality, and—it's true—you'll get up earlier and easier in the morning. You won't feel burdened and frustrated at the end of the day. You'll consciously bring more love and appreciation to your family members, and you'll even tend to eat more wisely and feel more sociable with the people at work. Why? Because you realize that it all serves you in a deeply meaningful way.

Words of Power

I do what I love and love what I do.

I am a beacon of light for the world.

I follow my mind's intuition and my heart's inspiration.

I make decisions rapidly and follow them patiently.

I prioritize my daily actions and focus on the top priority.

My reach extends throughout the world and beyond.

My purpose is crystal clear, and I am on target.

→ CHAPTER SIX ←

Unity: Your Family Treasures

"The family is one of nature's masterpieces."
— George Santayana

The concept of family can take many forms, depending on your personal definition. Of course, there are traditional versions, such as the nuclear family—Mom, Dad, and kids—as well as the extended family that includes grandparents, cousins, aunts, and uncles. But whether or not you have the traditional family, you may also have the collected family, which gets put together over the course of your life and consists of people who parent you, test you, cling to you, or admire you. These individuals may look up to you the way kids do, share honestly with you, or tease you just like a brother or sister would, and so on.

No matter if you live in the suburbs and drive a minivan to get advice from the elderly couple a few blocks over, or if you're a city dweller with a subway pass and close friends you always call in a pinch, you're part of a family. That's especially true when we define *family* as a group of people who are related because their personal lives intertwine—whether by blood or by choice. Everyone has times where they depend more on family by choice than on family by blood.

The family in all of its forms is as abundant with personal treasures as any of the other areas explored in this book. Becoming aware of the unity there—the harmony and order that already exist for you—is the first step to recognizing and experiencing the riches of a deeply fulfilling personal life, whether you think of your family members as just you and your romantic partner, or as a much bigger social network.

In their book *The HeartMath Solution,* stress researchers Doc Childre and Howard Martin wrote:

> Whether a biological family or an extended family of people attracted to each other based on heart resonance and mutual support, the word "family" implies warmth and a place where the core feelings of the heart can be nurtured. . . . A family made up of secure people generates a magnetic power that can get things done.

In this chapter, you'll learn more about how to evolve such a family for yourself—one that brings you treasured support and challenge and helps you live an amazing life. (Rather than characterizing these people as "secure," as Childre and Martin do, however, I'd be more likely to call them "loving." You'll understand why as you read on, since one of the family's greatest sources of richness lies in its contrasting opposites: security and risk, for example.) My own research and experience have shown that certain core feelings foster a family's awareness of unity, and they're essentially the same feelings

Childre and Martin (and their team of physicists, psychiatrists, and cardiologists) identified in 30 years of studying the "heart's intelligence." These foundational feelings are *love, appreciation,* and *care* for one another—the veins of gold running through each member of your family treasure.

Your Family Treasure #1: Equilibration

Childre and Martin included "happiness" in their list, too, and that's where we differ once more. In my opinion, "happily ever after" is indeed a fairy tale, a fantasy that people chase and never find. As I wrote earlier, happiness represents a lopsided perception.

One of the great fallacies of modern culture is that marriage and family are designed for happiness—that is, "Once you have these, you'll be happy!" Yet anyone who's paying attention knows that this isn't how it works because the truth is that you simply don't experience happiness without sadness.

Happy and sad are two sides of the proverbial coin. If you were able to stay on just one side of the coin and experience only one emotion, all action would stop. You'd stagnate or at the very least slow down your growth since maximum evolution occurs at the border of pleasure and pain. Mind the cliché: When you're green you're growing, and when you ripen, you rot—and happiness alone ripens you, while sadness acts as fertilizer. (Why else do you think we use the same word for manure as we do to describe events we see as negative? As they say, "S--t happens.")

Not only can you expect sadness to accompany happiness, but the more you fool yourself into expecting one to happen without the other alongside, the more frustrated you'll feel. Instead of being able to appreciate life for its complexity and balanced order, you'll get sucked into the illusion that everyone else has it "better" than you do.

So if you're not going to get pure happiness out of the deal, why get married? Why have a family? Why have relationships at all?

The superficial answer is that we're social creatures who desire intimate relationships. It's just how we're made: Part of human nature is to seek out others and create offspring. (There's that nudge to immortality, again.) Yet we must realize that our natural instincts serve us greatly—not by bringing us happiness, but by leading us to *equilibration.*

Your relationships balance you and make you aware of your wholeness. They help you recognize and love the parts of yourself that you previously thought were unlovable. Simply by showing you that these facets of yourself also exist in the people you love, your family members help you see and embrace that which is in you.

In other words, if individuals push your buttons, you can bet it's because they reflect a part of *you.* It's something that you don't like, and you pretend it doesn't exist in you. Yet the instant you recognize that *you have and display the very same trait* when someone else shows it, you can begin to more fully love that person. By doing so, you can more fully love yourself.

Isn't that a much more powerful experience than the pursuit of happiness—to love others for who they are and to love yourself in the process?

To help you arrive at this understanding, your family maintains a sense of balance in a startlingly precise way.

In any family, you can see how children express their parents' repressions. Every single thing that the parents disown or repress in their own selves pops up in their children's personas, affectations, and actions. Furthermore, each family's dynamic is designed to have peace and war—times when you cooperate with one another and times when you compete. Just as in all things, there are *both sides* to every family experience. A long time ago, I realized that I'm a Brahma, Vishnu, and Shiva all in one. I build or guide, I maintain, and I destroy. So do you and so does every member of your family.

If you're not open to this, and you're not aware of the two-sidedness of the human experience and of the paradoxical unity that it implies, then you're likely to believe in the myths of "broken dreams" and "broken hearts," which are false ideas that may victimize you. (For example, if someone you love has let you down in some way, you may have been projecting your values upon this person and expecting him or her to behave as you would or how you wish the individual would—that's generally the culprit in this situation. I'll talk more about that in the pages to come.) The price for buying into these illusions is the spectrum of imbalanced perceptions and feelings ranging from "disappointment" to "betrayal." But these are chimerical, make-believe monsters under the bed. When your lover doesn't live up to your expectations, it's not your heart that gets broken—*it's your fantasy of who you thought he or she "should" be that shatters*. When your son or daughter lives according to his or her values and not yours, it again *breaks the delusive fantasy.*

If you were to shine a light under the bed, you'd see that there are no monsters at all. The fantasies are made up of whom you think other people—particularly those closest to you—"ought" to be, not who they really are.

Vow to see and embrace both sides.

The wedding rituals of most cultures remind us to love one another in *wholeness* and *balance*. Worldwide, these sacred services acknowledge that in order to have lasting and loving relationships and create unifying bonds, the appreciation of both sides of life must be mastered. Consider the Buddhist vows:

> *In the future, happy occasions will come as surely as the morning.*
> *Difficult times will come as surely as the night.*

And the traditional Western vows:

> *For better, for worse,*
> *For richer, for poorer,*
> *In sickness and in health,*
> *To love and to cherish, till death do us part.*

These examples show that we can and do, occasionally, acknowledge that each person and every life has two sides: a self-righteous, virtuous, and optimistic side; and a "self-wrongeous," vicious, and pessimistic side. If one is publicly displayed, the other is privately experienced. No one, no matter how hard they try, can eliminate half of their own balanced nature.

Like a magnet, each of us has two sides. The more polarized these are, the more we become "manic" and "depressive," but the more integrated these sides are, the more balanced and consciously loving we become. Most people judge one aspect as good and the other as bad, yet whatever we attempt to avoid, we'll continue to run into in some form or fashion. On the other hand, when we acknowledge the duality of our natures, we realize our inherent unity. No one can escape this paradox. However, rising above this seeming contradiction is wisdom, and perceiving both sides as making a balanced masterpiece of love is simply seeing the magnificent order of the universe.

Your Family Treasure #2: Presence

During a seminar I was conducting, a woman told me that she couldn't possibly see how her mother was an equilibrating force in her life. "She abandoned me when I was four," the woman reported. A man sitting near her agreed: "My father died when I was six." Many people in the group had stories such as: "My parents divorced, and I never saw my dad after I was ten," "I never knew my grandparents," or "My brother ran away from home."

How can people fulfill their roles as equilibrators if they're not even in the picture anymore? How can they do anything for us if they've gone "missing"?

What you're about to read may challenge you at first, so I'm asking you now to think deeply, beyond your normal thoughts, because I guarantee that there's a great gift for you in this. It's been my observation after working with tens of thousands of people both in one-on-one consultations and in groups that *nothing is missing.* If you look carefully—and you may have to probe deeply into your memory banks to withdraw this treasure—when an individual departs your life, someone else (or many others) emerges to demonstrate the very traits that the departed person used to show you.

Not only have I observed this phenomenon in the lives of all the people who've worked with me through the years, but I've also experienced it firsthand, when there have been deaths in my family. When my father passed away more than a decade ago, *his* character traits immediately reemerged—partly through me and partly through certain other individuals around me. The same thing occurred when my mother passed more than five years ago—all of her traits were accounted for through a variety of people. It's quite remarkable! When someone departs from your life, whether it's through death or because the person moves away (physically or emotionally), there's truly no abandonment; there's simply transformation.

Can you begin to imagine how rich your life will be once you examine events with this in mind? Ordinary people live in illusions of gain and loss, hoping to get something they think they don't have—when in truth, they already do have it. Now is your chance to become an extraordinary person who realizes that your life lacks for nothing. Everything is present, but often it's in unrecognized forms.

Know that your soul mate is already here.

Nobody is missing a soul mate—all the traits that you're searching for in one partner are here in actuality throughout your life. The question is merely whether the soul mate is manifesting in one person or in many. One woman told me that she desperately wanted to find her soul mate, as she'd been waiting a long time for him to show up. I asked her to make a list of all the traits of a man she'd consider as her ideal mate. When she'd written down all the characteristics, I asked her, "You think all this is missing in your life?"

She emphatically said yes—there was no one in her life like this.

"Let's take a look," I ventured. "Where's the man in your life who is . . ."—I consulted her list—"your first trait here: 'extremely intelligent'?"

It took her only a moment to think of someone who fit this description. "But he isn't all those other things."

"Okay, I understand." I continued, "Who do you know who is 'humorous'?"

Once again someone immediately came to mind, as did other men who were good-looking, financially wealthy, enjoyed dancing, and so on. While she did this, she realized that there were already people in her life who possessed all of these traits, and she was actually interacting with them in business or in social circles. She began to see that everything she was looking for was already in her life in the form of many men—instead of just one. Her feelings of loss and lack calmed down, especially when she understood that her values had created this dispersed manifestation. In the past, she'd associated pain with having all this in one form (when she'd devoted herself to one man, she'd become unfocused in her business and had diminished her earnings and client base). The manifestation of her soul mate in many forms allowed her to have all the traits present in her life without dishonoring her highest values, which included a flourishing interior-design business.

Does this mean that she can't have one man who has all those characteristics—that is, meet her soul mate?

No, it doesn't. What I'm saying is that according to the truth of your values, you're creating your soul mate throughout your life—24 hours a day. All you need to do is stop and look carefully, and you'll find the form in which your values are manifesting. The moment you realize that what you value most isn't missing, it's like going to the bank with collateral: You're now able to *transform* those values into whatever you'd love to have in your life. Once you understand that nothing is missing and you already have whatever you seek, you have the power to alter your values and thereby change the form of the manifestation—into a single soul mate if that's what you'd love.

As soon as you see that nothing is missing, you open the gateways to the treasures of your life, which are present when you live without fearing loss, remorse, or pain.

Get rid of your "dysfunctional family."

An extension of this is giving up the notion of "dysfunctional families"—the idea that Mom or Dad harmed you or that other family members victimized you in some way—and instead, to embrace the idea of hidden function and order in every family. In some cases, only the soul knows the order; meanwhile, the bodily senses persist in perceiving the local disorder. That's why it's so easy to remain in the illusion of dysfunction, yet the truth of higher order is there for those who can push through the envelope of the senses and into the realm of the soul.

In any family, you can find a balance of character traits, and as I stated earlier, children express what their parents repress. Realize that across the members of a family or of any social system, including professional groups, church congregations, or what have you, there's a balance of character traits. For every assertive trait, there's a passive one; for every rational trait, there's an irrational one. Every person has a balance of positive and negative; and every family, when examined in its entirety, has each trait balanced by its complementary opposite.

To judge a family as dysfunctional is to be shallow in perspective and ignore how every person in the family contributes to the others' lives. This doesn't deny the fact that people experience some of the most intense feelings of pain from their family members and home lives; it's just that they will also encounter the heights of pleasure—and that every event and person in our lives has the potential to reveal to us a personal treasure chest of riches. **Each person in a family is needed exactly as he or she is for each of the other family members to learn to love unconditionally.**

If all the character traits of each family member were considered at once, a magnificent and hidden order would be revealed. The Demartini Method, which I present at my Breakthrough Experience seminar (and have detailed in previous books), can reawaken your understanding of this truth. When you open the heart . . . what is revealed is love—only love. So instead of blaming your family for anything, begin to look again. Look deeply. When you glimpse the hidden order—even if you can't see the entire matrix in all its glorious complexity—you get a glimmer of what it's like to no longer blame or succumb to self-dissociating excuses, and instead, you reside in the heart of love.

Your Family Treasure #3: Unconditional Love

You often hear nowadays that no one can love you until you love yourself, yet it's also true that you can't really love yourself if you don't open your heart to others. Fortunately, this isn't a chicken-and-egg type of question. **What's wisest is to open your heart to others.**

When you judge others as being either better or worse than you, you block your own self-love. The two are inseparable. As I said earlier, anyone around you whom you don't love right now represents a part of you that you haven't loved—a piece that you've disowned. Make it a point to recognize the ways in which you're like this person, and you'll find that it's not hard to actually love him or her, too. You'll come to love the individual . . . and yourself as well.

Forgo forgiving.

How do you know if you really love someone who has bothered you in the past and you're not just kidding yourself about it? You'll know when you no longer have an impulse to "forgive." When you see the truth, the magnificent order, there's no need for "I'm sorry." To unconditionally love is to see the instantaneous balance of the two illusory sides of the same event. For example, a family that's about to have an outdoor wedding would perceive a rainy day as "bad," but a farming family that has experienced a long drought, however, would perceive a rainy day as "good." One could say that it's both good and bad since it depends on how people perceive it. But the deeper truth is that it's neither, and people's judgments about the event don't actually reflect the real nature, which is only that it's raining. It's not good or bad; it just is.

When you judge your own or others' actions as bad and then say, "I'm sorry" or "I forgive you," you're acknowledging only one side of the event. (Keep in mind that this, in itself, isn't bad either; it's just an action from your mortal mind rather than a realization from your loving and immortal self.) Remaining balanced and grateful, your immortal self sees both sides simultaneously and only loves, responding simply with: "I love you and thank you."

Know that your judgments about what's good or bad are merely a reflection of your values. When something supports your belief system, you call it "good," but when something goes against it, you call it "bad." Anytime you do something that upholds your values, you label yourself "good" and build yourself up into self-righteousness; anytime you do something that goes against your value system, you put yourself down and inhabit a "self-wrongeous" persona.

The hierarchy of your values dictates how your mortal mind sees and attends to the world. It also dictates how you intend and act upon the world. **Attention and intention are based on your unique values.**

Link your love.

Consider a typical husband and wife in a mall, holding hands and window-shopping. Her highest values revolve around their children, and his revolve around business and finance. She feels drawn to the stores that sell goods for the kids: clothes, toys, educational items, and so on. "Oh honey, let's stop in there!" she might say.

In that moment, the wife has developed "attention surplus order," but the husband has developed "attention deficit disorder." As they enter the store, he may even start to yawn, just as she's starting to dawn—lighting up at all the choices she has for making their children's lives "better" in her view. As he sees how excited she is, he exercises patience and waits for her to finish.

Then they continue to stroll, and he pulls her into the computer shop with the latest technology for business. In no time, they've reversed roles: She's yawning and finds herself saying, "I'll meet you outside in 30 minutes. I'm just going across the way to . . ."

As long as the husband doesn't start wishing and expecting his wife to live according to *his* values instead of hers, and the wife doesn't start fantasizing that he would be a "better husband" if he were more interested in their kids' clothing, they'll be able to appreciate one another's company in the mall. More important, as long as the couple focuses on how their differences actually complement one another, they'll be able to see how they're connected in love—an unconditional love, where each honors the others' value system and recognizes that it's just as valid as his or her own.

One highly effective way of acknowledging and honoring complementary differences is through the exercises that I've already shared with you in this book. Just as you learned to link your values with the activities and mission of your business, you can also link your values to those of your loved ones.

Start by giving your loved ones the values-elicitation exercise to complete (see Chapter 3, "Divinity: Your Spiritual Treasures"), or refer to it yourself and come up with an assessment of their values on your own. Now take the time to link your values to theirs.

Write down your top five values on one side of a piece of paper, and then on the other side, list the top five values of a loved one. Now think of at least five ways that the other person's highest value helps you fulfill your highest value. Then jot down at least five ways that your top value helps the other person fulfill their top value—the *first* on your loved one's list.

Go on and note five ways that your top value helps the other person fulfill their *second* highest value; then continue on down the list so that you're creating hundreds of cross-connections. (For a detailed example of this exercise along with sample responses, please see my book *The Heart of Love*.)

Your Family Treasure #4: Caring

In any relationship, there will be times of clear communication and miscommunication. That's partly because each of us has such a tendency to project our own values onto others. If you don't take the time to link your values to those you love (as I just described), you can get pulled into the dance of self-righteousness and exaggeration, expecting others to live according to your values instead of their own.

Have you ever caught yourself saying things such as, "Oh, he's got a lot of potential"? You might as well be saying, "Have I got plans for you! Won't you be just great when I get through with you?" This sets both of you up for frustration: If you tell the person your plans and expectations, you're probably going to be perceived as domineering—and the person is likely to wonder, "Why won't you just let me be? Why am I not good enough for you just the way I am?" If he or she goes along with it and minimizes what's true for him or her, the relationship will diminish. On the other hand, if you launch a covert makeover, then you're creating a guessing game where you don't reveal your expectations, and every time the other person doesn't live up to your hopes, you dole out punishment. Again the person is minimized—and the relationship diminished.

This dismissal of someone else's values can be called *careless*. If you were to minimize yourself, beat yourself up for *not* being someone you aren't, try to inject another person's values into your life, and judge yourself lacking somehow, we could call this being *careful*.

It's much less complicated and far more loving for you to be *caring* instead, and simply remember that people have their own sets of values. You and everyone else you meet wants to be loved for who they are, which includes those values—what's important to *them*. If you project your values and minimize who they are, this creates resistance; if you inject their values and minimize who you are, this creates resentment. Who doesn't want to be cherished for being *exactly* who they are? Isn't this the definition of unconditional love?

When you quit projecting your values, you can stop having affairs with fantasy figures and start being *in love*. You can stop trying to "fix" people, which is futile anyway. (Look—you can't even change yourself most of the time, let alone other people. Have you ever tried to "be positive" for a day? What happened? Before the end of the day, no doubt something happened that "made you mad"—or "negative." Even if you smiled your way through it, you were just fooling yourself.) Every person has two sides and if you attempt to eradicate one, it's like laying out the welcome mat for circumstances and people to bring that suppressed side into your life. You know the cliché: Whatever you resist persists.

Four primary obstacles prevent your access to the true riches of family, or unconditional love:

1. Holding on to false concepts or myths about love (some of which you've read in this chapter and all of which are covered in my book *The Heart of Love*)

2. Imagining that the universe in which we live is random, one-sided, chaotic, and disordered

3. Not recognizing what pushes your buttons of fear and guilt

4. Developing and displaying false personas with self-righteous and "self-wrongeous" attitudes

The simplest and easiest step to take to recover the treasures of love is to balance your mind's perceptions. This will reconnect you with the soul, return you to a state of gratitude, and open your heart to allow your true love—for yourself and for others—to shine. This state of gratitude can be accomplished by asking yourself these two essential questions whenever you're confronted by a "button pushing" trait—whether you perceive it as negative or positive—in someone else:

1. *Where and when have I done or not done that, and what is its blessing?*

2. *Where and when have I done or not done that, and what is its drawback?*

By looking at life through the eyes of an observer—one who can see both sides of each person and event and can also see oneself—you'll begin to acknowledge the magnificence of what is, simply as it is, in the world around you. This compassion enables you to expand your relationships beyond your immediate surroundings. Unconditional love is unlimited; and it radiates from you as an individual to your family—and onward throughout your city, state, nation, and world—continuing out to your stars, galaxy, and the universe.

Words of Power

Love is all there is—all else is an illusion.

I love myself exactly as I am.

I give and receive love each day, and I love it.

I am unconditionally loving.

No matter what happens, I know it is a lesson in love.

Within me and around me, there is nothing but love.

My love reigns supreme over all
of my other imbalanced emotions.

CHAPTER SEVEN

Leadership: Your Social Treasures

"There are [people], who, by their sympathetic attractions, carry nations with them, and lead the activity of the human race."
— Ralph Waldo Emerson

Embracing support *and* challenge equally is one of the hallmarks of great leadership. No matter what occurs, knowing that you can say, "That's fine because it serves me" lends you tremendous power. In fact, your ability to do this determines the reach of your leadership. If you can have only a few people question or confront you before it starts rattling you, you'll lead in a smaller way than if you can have a billion people do so while you consistently maintain your vision. Great leaders can handle enormous challenges and still hold fast to what they know is true.

In one way or another, you're already a leader. You may lead your family, school, community, or a larger political arena; or you may be the head of an organization, your workplace, or some subsidiary of it. Whatever it is, wherever you lead, acknowledge the power you hold right now. To minimize yourself and exaggerate the importance of others diminishes your ability to direct and control the difference you make in the world. Recognizing the richness of your own leadership ability, on the other hand, starts an amazing cascade of opportunities and energies flowing to and from you.

All the rules we have in our world today emanate from people who have power—in other words, whoever has the most power makes the rules. If you make yourself small and don't acknowledge the full degree of your own power and leadership (that is, if you don't recognize what you're truly capable of achieving and go out and do something magnificent), you're living in a world of "should's," "ought to's," and "supposed to's"—all dictated by someone else. But you can change that right now, simply by standing up to your full measure and perceiving yourself as a loving and wise leader. Start to live in inspiration and "love to's" while discovering the real treasure of you.

Your Social Treasure #1: Association

More than 30 years ago, I made a list of people I would have loved to meet: great leaders, renowned thinkers, celebrities, and individuals who were leaving their mark on history. I did this because I was and still am a firm believer in the idea that what you write down—what you look at, think about, visualize, and affirm—you end up manifesting.

However, at the time my list seemed like quite a stretch, because I had no idea how I might go about meeting these people—many of whom I thought were considerably out of my league. I just had it in my mind that I'd love to do it, and I can now tell you that in the three decades since I first set pen to paper, I've met every one of them! Because I defined exactly whom I'd love to meet, somehow I found myself eating in the same restaurants with these individuals, sharing the stage with them at some events, bumping into them at social gatherings, and even sitting next to them a few times during airplane flights.

It's as if you draw people into your life by thinking of them. If you're in business and you focus on your clients (that is, your innermost dominant thought is of them), then *their* innermost dominant thought becomes you. You "somehow" resonate and they come to you—what you seek tends to seek you.

I believe that our innermost dominant thought does become our outermost tangible reality. If you have a vision to meet great people, you'll end up attracting the individuals, places, things, ideas, and events—synchronicities—that will help orchestrate your actually meeting them.

You may be thinking, *What was the point of meeting them?* My experience is that if you're regularly in the presence of people who've impacted the world—those who are leaving their mark on history—the encounter helps you recognize the great store of treasures that you already possess to do the same.

Make your own list.

Write down the names of powerful leaders, distinguished achievers, ingenious minds, or celebrities you'd love to meet or associate with. Read your list daily and believe in the possibilities—and watch what happens.

However, you can't do this without also putting the wheels of the universe in motion. No matter where you are in life right now, begin to associate with the great immortals by writing their names on a piece of paper that you keep near to you. Their names alone resonate in such a way that you will attune to them; and by doing so, you'll help bring out your own magnificence.

Right now, choose 50 men and women you believe might make a significant difference in the world, regardless of their field of endeavor. Be sure to include your own name.

Read stories of powerful world leaders and celebrities.

When you immerse yourself in the life stories of the great people of our time and historic figures who've left a lasting impact, you infiltrate your mind with alternative thoughts that direct you to ideas of leadership. The biographies of these people are filled with decisions that dictated the course of their lives and, in many cases, directed the course of history.

If you expose yourself to these people, you soon come to the realization that being a successful leader means having the ability to make meaningful decisions quickly and hold them persistently. Leadership and power come to those who have the courage to not only listen to both sides of any experience, but also to attend to the true inner leader within to inspire purposeful action.

By reading about the lives of these remarkable men and women, you awaken the powerful leader within you. You relate to their experiences and feel what they felt. You also build courage—and it reveals itself so that you can lead your own personas and fragmented parts toward a meaningful purpose. Those who lead others lead themselves first.

You'll discover the genuine power that lies within you by studying other leaders. Earlier in the book, you read about a consultant who put his mind to attracting Fortune 500 clients. He was successful because he recognized that *he* also possessed all the traits that he admired in these powerful businesspeople. Similarly, as you read biographies, consider the ways in which you're just like Albert Einstein, for example, or Michael Jordan, Bill Gates, Abraham Lincoln, Mahatma Gandhi, or any of the other thousands of people we recognize as outstanding examples of various kinds of leadership.

Find the leader within.

Every time you find something you admire in the life of someone great, write it down. Study these people until you can see that you possess the same qualities they do. **If they can do what they've done, so can you!** That's a great affirmation.

This is the opposite of being a "fan." Fans put someone on a pedestal because they imagine that just because they feel admiration, that person is somehow different from them. No! What I'm asking you to do is to turn your admiration into something else altogether: a realization that this person presents a unique embodiment of the exact same traits you already possess!

Sometimes people who attend my seminars or read my books become temporarily infatuated with me. They start to think I'm remarkable in some way and praise me: "Oh John! You're wonderful, and you know so much, and you're this, and you're that . . ." (Of course, people also reprimand me, but that's not the point of this story.)

My response is generally the same: "Listen, I'm just like you. Right now, I'm doing my job, which I love doing. My values aren't better or worse than your values—they're just different. If you think you see something in me that you admire, stop right now and find out where you have it, too, because if you put me on a pedestal, you minimize yourself. And if you minimize yourself, then the very message that I'm trying to share isn't getting through to you. Really look and you'll see that I'm a reflection of you. *If you spot it, you've got it!* Own whatever you see in me. By looking carefully, you'll discover where your remarkable traits or actions already exist, all according to your unique hierarchy of values. You're a magnificent human being with your own vital energies, amazing talents, and vision."

Everyone has a leader inside. Own the traits you admire in others and you'll resonate with those leaders, too. You'll probably also draw them into your life.

Develop a magnetic personality.

Magnetism fills a great leader. These people radiate confidence, and their certainty moves others into action. This magnetism arises automatically in a being who's inspired and will grow in one who's clear about his or her mission.

Read acclaimed books about human magnetism; other leaders have done so, and the wisdom gleaned from those who've gone before helps the aspiring leaders of today. One contemporary book I recommend is

Instantaneous Personal Magnetism, by Edmund Shaftesbury. It's a 400-page book read by many notable figures since it was published in 1926. Of course, there are several other excellent books on this subject worth considerable study, but this one is fascinating reading and can give you numerous insights on the development of a magnetic character. Visit your library or bookstore and start your own research into this powerful body of knowledge.

Take a little trip.

Or take a big one. As I mentioned earlier, visiting the cities or civilizations where great leaders have resided awakens awe in the magnificence of ancient worlds and their peoples. By visiting these places, you get a feeling for the power and leadership that must have been in effect when they were flourishing. The incredible organization that was needed even then is astounding. To manage all the many factions of a society takes true genius, and to maintain leadership among so many takes true inspiration. You can't experience these cultures without having flashes of déjà vu, for their vibrations seem to revive remnants of memories buried deep within your genetic code. Your immortal self knows more than just what's provided by its mortal form—and it has a higher capacity to resonate with powerful people, places, and their leaders through time.

A friend of mine says that she's always most susceptible to this kind of experience whenever she puts her hand on a banister, or her foot on the same steps, where people from other times and places have walked. She doesn't attribute this to any kind of "psychic" power, but she does acknowledge that something wonderful happens in her psyche. These moments spark the imagination—they fire the soul. In historic places, from France's palaces to Mexico's Mayan ruins and to slave quarters in the U.S. southern states, she has found herself in tears, smiling from ear to ear, or simply awestruck.

Whether you travel abroad or stay closer to home makes little difference, since it's become so easy to visit famous leaders' homes or palaces. In the United States, you can tour not only the White House but also the former homes of many inspiring Presidents, such as Thomas Jefferson's Monticello, George Washington's Mount Vernon estate (which is within driving distance of Monticello), James Madison's Montpelier, and James Monroe's Ash Lawn-Highland. Of course, innovative scientists, inventors, and celebrities of all sorts are also within your reach.

If you can't visit the actual places, re-creations in film and virtual tours online still serve the purpose, which is to expand the possibilities in your own mind, stoke your creative imagination, and acquaint you with the ideas and goals of people whose inspiration drove their lives.

Often great leaders surrounded themselves with material treasures: fine art and architecture, beautiful clothes, magnificent vehicles for transportation, and stunning gardens. Most people love to peek at the "lifestyles of the rich and famous" from any era. It's as if every one of us has a calling for the finer accoutrements of life. By visiting homes studded with these things, greater motivation and broader dreams can be inspired.

Realize that your immortal self is drawn to beauty. It's attracted to it and is inspired by anything that stems from a similar nature. When you surround yourself with masterpieces that arose from inspiration, you can't walk away without also being inspired yourself. There's tremendous power in an inspiring thought—and incredible beauty in the mind of one who lives surrounded by such creativity.

True leaders focus their followers on the greater and more refined directions in life. Although each follower may be on a lower social level, an inspiring and powerful leader will elevate them to a higher octave. Only false leaders seek to keep others down. Until you pass the torch, you don't receive the light.

Your Social Treasure #2: Permission

When I was a teenager, I used to panhandle, and I'd go into restaurants looking for leftover food on the tables. So I know what it's like to assume I have "nothing." But now I also know what it's like to associate with some amazing people, who are global leaders with global power. The difference between where I was then and where I am now is simply that I had the courage to acknowledge that I *could* resonate with these people, even if I didn't know how to do it at the time, and that I have those same traits.

Perhaps you haven't given yourself that permission. Why not do it right now?

No matter who you are and what you do in your everyday life, you're already touching the world. Take a moment right now to think about how your actions impact the rest of the people who live on this earth with you. Whether it's in your job—through a product or service—or in your larger life, think of how you reach someone else, give others opportunities, and spread some spark of your soul across the world.

Realize that *you're worthy of global functioning, and give yourself permission to go for it.* You deserve to be magnificent—to be someone who makes a difference. No one wakes up in the morning and desires to shrink. We're here to grow, expand, and fulfill—and share our tremendous riches within.

Say yes to greater social contacts.

You've already made a list of 50 people you'd love to meet someday. Now think about who's already in your life: individuals you've met or those who live right in your own hometown. Who are the people you'd love to hang out with? They're the ones who will *make you stretch.* Think about who can help your awareness grow, who will pull more out of you than you'd pull out of yourself on your own.

Now make a list of what you can do for each of these people—not what they can do for you, but whatever you can do to contribute to *their* lives. What can you do for each of these people, according to what you know about their values? If you help someone according to his or her values, that person is more likely to appreciate your company.

Become an authority.

As a child, the rules of your life are set by your parents. In your teen years, you sometimes defy your parents and start thinking independently, although the rules still come from someone other than you: social peers, schoolmates, and eventually colleagues at work. At some point, you may decide to go into business for yourself and become aware of what it's like to set your own rules. Neither parents, teachers, nor bosses have power over you; and you've already transcended some of your friends. But instead of a parent or boss making the rules, as a business owner, you now must abide by the laws and restrictions of the city.

Eventually, you may grow a company that's citywide and become friends with the local politicians; those people no longer rule you because you're participating in their game and know how to play it. Now the state government rules. Eventually, you may grow into a multistate business, and the state won't want to lose you because you employ lots of people. At this point, you have influence at the state level, and the national government rules you. If you get to the point of a multinational corporation, where you have influence across continents, you start to deal with world organizations. And when you get beyond that, you're the sage—now only the universal laws govern you.

People at the top are the most actualized and free, and those at the bottom have all the pressure of multiple levels of "rulers." (There's a clever, slightly off-color saying about this: "Monkeys at the bottom of the tree look up and see a bunch of a--holes, while monkeys at the top look down and see a bunch of smiling faces.") Where do you want to play in the game of life? If you hang out at the bottom, you're more likely to bow down to other people's values and live under perceived authority—unable to automatically pursue your dreams and self-actualize. You're not free in this position, and you need to constantly seek permission from a higher authority.

If you're willing to continually empower yourself and keep growing by loving people . . . if you love yourself enough to continue honoring your vision . . . if you keep expanding your mind by educating yourself and empowering yourself in all areas, then eventually you rise in the system! Instead of subordinating yourself to some perceived authority and value system, you *create* the value system that rules your life and dictates your destiny.

Never a big fan of authority, Albert Einstein half joked: "To punish me for my contempt for authority, fate made me an authority myself." His observation was wise, too. Einstein was unwilling to submit to some perceived authorities just because they held the common "wisdom" of the day. In addition, his commitment to keep looking at the laws of the universe until he saw *beyond authority,* immortalized him as a genius of universal laws.

As a leader, you allow yourself to receive, to serve, and to climb and rise—all because it's your nature to do so. Nobody gets up in the morning and thinks, *I want less power* or *I want to be under someone else's thumb!* When we watch a culture that has experienced disempowerment under the tyranny of dictators rise up and break through to exist as a free nation, we applaud. The same thing can occur in individual lives. Each of us deserves to live a free life in which we can say, "I do what I love and love what I do. I love the people who do it with me. I love sharing my life's inspiration with others and inspiring other people." That's freedom . . . and that's leadership.

Everybody leads somebody, and everybody follows, too. Dig deep for your treasures of leadership. Find your inner soul's authority, and realize that you're a leader with the power to effect profound change in other people's lives. No matter what level you're playing at right now, and no matter what level you're planning to live on, know that you have leadership! You have the skills and the power. Honor that!

Your Social Treasure #3: Mission and Message

Unlike my earlier years in school, by the time I was a premed student, I began accruing honors and top grades. At the time, I'd decided to become a chiropractor because I loved the philosophy of this branch of the healing arts. It's founded on the belief in a universal intelligence or wisdom that permeates everything and is innately inside everyone. Each of us can access this wisdom and are held back from doing so only by false and disempowering beliefs.

As part of my newfound inspiration, I was a voracious reader and serious student. At one point I was ridiculed, mainly because I was so diligent that it had started to reflect on other students' performance. (Yes, the same young man who had struggled with reading and had failed a class just a few years earlier was now messing with the grading curve by setting a new standard for getting an A!) So I was a bit of a menace in my classes.

For graduation, however, my effort earned me the opportunity to speak to my classmates. I stood before them and said, "I want to be a leader in our profession, to make a contribution to each of you, to keep the spiritual philosophy of chiropractic alive among us and across the world." Today, I speak before thousands of chiropractors each year. I've dedicated myself to this amazing field because I believe we're looking past the true cause of healing—thinking that it's something that comes only from the outside, when in truth the real healer is inside each of us. Whenever anything "out there" works, it's because it somehow inspires the healing power "in here" to do its job. There's such power within each of us!

It's probably clear to you that I still feel strongly about this, and it's become a part of my evolving mission and message. So even though my life has taken its own meandering course, it's always been on track—according to the purpose I saw for myself that first time I heard Paul Bragg speak.

Listen to your heart, and you'll hear your own mission and message for the world. This may be tied to your professional life, or it may not. Either way, those with the clearest sense of purpose—as directed by the soul—become the leaders of the world. They're the people who sound a message so clear that others are drawn to it and inspired to join in to change the course of history.

The few who have the courage to listen to and act upon their mission lead the many. There's nothing wrong with being a follower, though; in fact, it's a prerequisite to becoming a great leader. The difference is that true leaders learn to heed their soul's inner voice, while the many ordinary followers in the world just get in line behind others' voices.

You'll find your prime area of leadership. It may be in the domain of your home life, spiritual life, profession, or even in your hobby. Wherever you feel called to lead, listen to your soul and obey. This gives you a clear mission—and from that, you formulate and communicate a concise message. You become unstoppable! The power of an idea whose time has come is explosive. Your soul has such an idea, and it knows the right time to inspire you to action. Perhaps that's why you're reading this book.

Keep quiet. Listen.

Meditate every day on your purpose or mission. Reread the purpose statement you've written for yourself, and contemplate its significance. Ask your greater self for guidance on how to make this immortal idea become a reality. Listen and follow wisely.

Your Social Treasure #4: Commitment

Magical events occur when you add commitments to your actions, and such commitments emerge spontaneously when your mission is aligned perfectly with your highest values. By making a promise to your mission, vision, or calling, the entire universe seems to align with you in order to assist you. Your commitment shows that you're truly ready for action, and it seems as if the universe will test you until you make a strong declaration. This is why it's so powerful to have written down your purpose statement and continue to read it every day. It's a kind of pact with your higher or more inspired self—one that you reseal each day to ensure that you're ready.

When I was 17 years old and wrote my own mission statement for the first time, I had a feeling that it would change the course of my destiny. I felt such a profound influence after hearing Paul Bragg speak that I wanted to follow in his footsteps—studying the laws of the universe and relating them to the body, mind, and spirit as he had. I knew then that I wanted to travel the world and be handsomely paid for it as I researched these laws. I wanted to become a healer, philosopher, writer, and speaker; and I wanted to dedicate my life to the study of the true and immortal source of creative evolution and life. For the gift of his example, I'm very grateful. He was a powerful influence to me at a time when I was ready to be inspired by such leadership. And he's still an inspiration to me: I dream of the day when I'm 93 years young and can share my message with some 17-year-old man or woman and change a life in the same way that Paul Bragg transformed mine.

From that moment forward, I experienced numerous hurdles. I've felt like giving up on my dream once, and I was considerably challenged many times. But my greater self—the part of me that connects with my most inspired essence—has just kept on picking me up and polishing me to make me shine more fully.

Whenever I have renewed my vitality or commitment, more thoroughly aligned my actions to my highest values, redoubled my persistence, and decided not to give up, I've experienced a surge of energy that moves me even more swiftly toward the realization of my dream. Commitment to a soul-guided mission is what breeds immortal power. It expands your lungs and provides you with the breath of immortal life. It's taken me around the world; and when you make such a commitment, it will expand your horizons and bring you to the riches of a fully treasured life.

Your Social Treasure #5: Influence

In order to expand your leadership, you must open your mind. Without consistently overcoming mental boundaries, you become circumscribed by your self-imposed limitations. You *can't* manifest your dreams in any realm or sphere of influence that you haven't mentally transcended. Yet you *can* transcend your current "circle" of thought. As Emerson wrote in an 1841 essay: "The life of man is a self-evolving circle, which, from a ring imperceptibly small, rushes on all sides outwards to new and larger circles, and that without end."

When you expand your reach of mental resources beyond your existing sphere, you break through to a new concentric sphere of living. Your creations are born of this new mental vision and its resources.

Your soul puts no boundaries on your visions or resources. Therefore, the more you listen to your soul, the more powerful your creations will be. Truly inspired and lasting leaders listen to and view the unbounded messages and visions of their soul. They grow like a tree's branches toward the sun—ever upward and outward. These visionaries make a difference in the world around them because their soul calls them to an astronomical mission. Remember what I mentioned earlier:

To make a difference in yourself, you must have a community vision.

To make a difference in your community, you must have a city vision.

To make a difference in your city, you must have a state/province vision.

To make a difference in your state/province, you must have a national vision.

To make a difference in your nation, you must have a world vision.

To make a difference in your world, you must have a stellar vision.

May your soul guide you to such a profound vision that you have tears of inspiration in your eyes just contemplating it. May it stretch your boundaries to the stars, allowing you to shine with the radiance of love.

Words of Power

I am filled with the power of love—
the greatest of all powers.

I have a mission, I have a message, and I lead wisely.

I am magnetic, and I draw to myself magnificent people.

People will do whatever it takes to be in my presence.

My purpose is so clear that others can actually see it.

The world is my playground, and
I am a winner in the game of life.

I am a born leader, and my destiny is greatness.

AFTERWORD

"Heroes take journeys, confront dragons, and discover the treasure of their true selves."
— Carol Pearson

Reading a book like this can have the effect of energizing you and helping you do what you already know you'd love to do, but just haven't given yourself permission to undertake. It can also help you gain insights into your character, purpose, personality, and immortal essence that spur you toward greater heights—even if you were already "on the path." If this is where you are right now, you have my sincere support for the tasks you have before you—and my challenge to follow through with your whole heart.

On the other hand, you may find yourself feeling that you have an enormous list of things you "should" do. It's as if you no longer have the excuse of ignorance to put off pursuing what's most important to you, yet you're still sulking or beating yourself up because you think it's all just "too much." Beware. Feelings of "should" and "ought to" won't get you anywhere, as they're just expressions of fear and guilt. And if you read the Introduction to this book, you know that those are the only two things that could stop you from revealing all seven of your secret treasures—and from unearthing all the riches of your mind, heart, soul, and body.

Here's a solution: If you're feeling overwhelmed by all the to-dos I've offered in this book, *pick one area,* one treasure, that you feel sincerely inspired to polish to its most brilliant shine. Focus on that. Make a checklist for yourself of the exercises and other practical suggestions in the corresponding chapter, and then get started today.

Will you begin by digging into your vocational treasures, ensuring that you do what you love and love what you do?

Will it be your mental treasures, uncovering your genius?

How about your physical treasures? Are you ready to reacquaint yourself with the immortal messages of the body?

Maybe you'll begin with your spiritual treasures, reconnecting with a divine purpose and quest that will inspire you for the rest of your days.

Or perhaps you'll dig into your financial treasures, and discover the wealth that you already possess. In time, you'll grow your material riches beyond what you've ever imagined!

Is it the right moment to discover all of your family treasures—not only enlightening yourself, but perceiving and enhancing the unity of those around you?

Just what might you accomplish if you decided to uncover greater social treasures and unleash your wise leadership, offering your service of love to the world?

Choose one area that speaks to your soul and moves

your heart so that when you ponder its potential brilliance—by taking a few moments to imagine the fulfillment of your own magnificent possibilities—you find yourself brushing away tears of awe and gratitude. And then, whatever area you choose, take it piece by piece. Make a checklist, apply it to your calendar, and just keep following through with persistence. Use the words of power you find at the end of the corresponding chapter to keep your mind focused on the ultimate reality you're manifesting.

For now, concentrate on this area, and make it your pet project. Sometime in the future, you'll choose another area—and then another. In time, you'll have embraced all seven of your secret treasures and have introduced them to the world, too.

From One to Many and Back Again

In my studies of philosophy, religion, and science, I came across the term *logos,* which has many meanings but essentially represents the source of all existence. The Greek philosopher Heracleitus, for example, said, "Listening not to me but to the Logos, it is wise to agree that all is one." The Jewish philosopher Philo used it to mean the creative principle. The Gospel of John calls Jesus "the Logos," often translated as "the Word"; and this passage alone has spurred centuries of discourse about the unified nature of the Christian trinity. Ancient philosophers who were well versed in all areas spoke of the *logos*—a cohesive field of intelligence.

Today, we have specialization, so the *logos* that the great philosophers studied has fractionated into the various disciplines and "ologies" we have today: theology, biology, psychology, sociology, and so on. If you were to study all the disciplines, however, you'd discover the common threads that make up the *logos*. That's why I wanted to tackle so many pieces of the puzzle myself—I wanted to see more of the whole picture. Likewise, as you take on each of the seven areas outlined in this book, you'll come to see the *logos* of your own life.

One thing that I've gained absolute certainty about in my studies is the piece of wisdom I shared with you earlier: As I was hitchhiking to California, a bum on the street in El Paso told me that the essence of all life is love, wisdom, and appreciation.

Consider this: If you had only 24 hours to live, what would you do? If you're like most people I meet, you'd communicate your love and gratitude to the people who have contributed to your life. And would you love to be loved and appreciated for who you are? Yes! Of course! Wisdom is the ability to appreciate other individuals, and share your light and love with them. This is the development of the human consciousness.

Don't wait for 24-hour notice. Start living this way today, and dig for the treasure. *You will find it.* You may have to throw out some junk along the way, and you might break a few shovels as you go . . . just keep on digging.

You radiate brilliance already, for you're a genius with an immortal soul. You connect with the spiritual source and deserve the financial abundance that comes from doing what you love and loving what you do. You possess the power to lead in both small and great endeavors.

Take the journey, confront the dragons, and discover the treasure of your true self. May the luster of all your riches within light up the world.

APPENDIX A

The Demartini Method®
Instructions and Blank Worksheets

As any treasure hunter will tell you, one of the first rules of the game is being willing to *dig*. And if you've got a map, so much the better. That's what this section offers you: the tools to dig and a map to help you uncover all seven of your secret treasures.

I've included the first two parts of The Demartini Method®, sides A and B of the worksheet. This will assist you with initiating personal excavation, and you'll certainly notice results after completing just this first part of the process. You'll get a serious look at what's inside that treasure chest!

When you're ready to dig even deeper, know that there's more for you. You can access additional elements of The Demartini Method in my earlier books *The Heart of Love* (which primarily addresses relationship issues) and *The Breakthrough Experience* (detailing the entire method). You can also observe the process in person by attending my live event of the same title, *The Breakthrough Experience.*

Let's get digging!

Step 1: Choose Your Subject

Start by picking a person whom you have an imbalanced perspective of—that is, someone you have lopsided feelings, beliefs, or thoughts about. The first time you use this method, you're wise to pick a subject who has a serious charge for you, whether it's "positive" or "negative."

Many people have used The Demartini Method to bring balance to situations and relationships. For example, some individuals have used this process when they thought they "needed" to get married to someone because their betrothed was entirely "perfect and powerful" (and, by contrast, they falsely considered themselves to be only "flawed and weak"); others have successfully used the method to deal with intense feelings of rage, sadness, fear, and grief. One woman who completed The Demartini Method was able to resolve and ultimately feel gratitude about a situation that most people would find unimaginable: She had survived the devastating 2004 Southeast Asian tsunami, but her husband and son had been swept out to sea. And a man I know, who's quite accomplished and has what he calls "lots of opportunities for egomania" tells me that this helps keep him from getting his head "swelled to the size of the moon." These are just a few of the thousands of possible applications. I know you'll find many that work for you, too.

You might start by considering each of the areas we've covered in this book. Is there someone whom you identify with each of your seven secret treasures: genius (mental), immortality (physical), divinity (spiritual), wealth (financial), power (vocational), unity (familial), and leadership (social)? Do you think that you know someone who exemplifies or embodies the "highest" and "greatest" traits in this area? If you're truly committed to fully revealing your own brilliance in each of these categories, then you're wise to choose a person for each one, and complete a separate set of worksheets for every individual. Just be sure to do Side A first and Side B second.

In this book, I've also talked about using this method to deal with someone who pushes your buttons, ticks you off, and gets under your skin. If you decide to begin with this part (and there's no reason not to—it's your choice, and the method works great regardless of where you start), then in that case, begin with Side B, and then complete the Side A worksheet.

As I said, this is the map—just like the clichéd phrase "X Marks the Spot." The questions in this worksheet show you exactly where you need to go to completely recover all seven of your secret treasures in order to fully recognize all of the riches within.

Step 2: Set Aside Some Time for Yourself

This isn't a five-minute fix-it. You may need an hour or two, and you may even need to stretch this process over a day or so. You might feel tired and want to take a break—then come back to what you were doing. That's perfectly fine.

There's no "trick" to doing this process "right." Just follow the map and answer the questions with as much honesty as you can possibly muster; your truth is your most precious tool in the quest for your personal treasure.

So stick with it! If you begin to feel tired, overwhelmed, or frustrated, just remember *that's the time to push through,* because the other side is where all the richness resides. Get inspired when you start to feel stretched by this method: It's the moment before your breakthrough. Imagine yourself as an explorer who's just about to find the secret door that opens to an amazing hidden cache of priceless treasures.

Step 3: Use the Forms as a Map to Guide You

As I stated in Step 1, if you've chosen a subject you *admire* (infatuation), start with Side A first; if you're working with a subject you *resent,* begin with Side B. No matter which side you're working on, keep in mind that the more *precise and concise* you are, the more useful your results will be. Generalities and elaborations slow down the process, but specifics and brevity speed it up.

Detailed instructions for filling in the worksheets follow.

Step 4: Go Till You Find the Gold

As you work on The Demartini Method, ignore the impulse to give up and decide that it can't work for you because . . . [fill in the blank]. I don't care what your "fill in the blank" is—I can assure you that it's simply not true. Don't stop once you've started! Keep going until you can sincerely answer *yes* to the questions I've provided to help you determine whether you're done with each column.

You can do this, just as thousands of other people have done before you.

How will you know when you've truly completed The Demartini Method? Over and over again, I've seen the same signs in people as they finish this method. It's as if they've found something they've been looking for, yet it was always right there inside.

The most immediate and noticeable result of this profound discovery is a feeling of brightness, weightlessness, and gratitude—it's your brilliance that's breaking through. You may find yourself welling up and experiencing something like this. . . .

— **Tears of inspiration.** People cry when they're moved by their inspiration. This isn't sadness or elation, though; it's balanced gratitude and love. Tears come when you recognize the magnificence of the world in which you live and the incredible radiance of the riches within.

— **Fearlessness and guiltlessness.** There's no impulse to apologize, seek an apology, or confer forgiveness. You've shed the lopsided perceptions of fear and guilt that might have led you to think that things would be any "better" if they were different.

— **Unconditional gratitude and love.** You no longer wish for anything different, and you love what is. The only words on your lips are "Thank you," and "I love you." Of course, there may also come a time when there's nothing to be said, and all that remains is to embrace the person you love.

— **Silence inside and out.** The usual mind chatter silences, and only your soul speaks. In moments like this, there are no words.

— **Uplifted head and eyes.** Having done this method in more than 50 countries around the world, I've seen one thing happen everywhere I go: People raise their eyes as if they're looking to something greater above and beyond. You may look up and say, "Thank you, universe," because you realize that before this moment, you didn't understand how beautifully it was ordered.

Instructions for Side A

(*Note:* A copy of the form used for this exercise is included at the end of this Appendix.)

Side A of The Demartini Method is designed to balance any *infatuation* you may have. It helps you:

- Identify the traits you admire or perceive as positive
- Acknowledge that those traits aren't just outside of you; they exist in you, too
- See how each one can actually be a drawback, realizing that so-called negatives are also present
- Recognize what benefits might occur if the person or situation were magically reversed

This brings balance, revealing the magnificence in both the world around you and the riches within you.

Column 1

— *Purpose:* You're about to pinpoint the specific, most positively charged human traits, actions, or inactions that draw or attract you—the ones that "hook" you and/or bring out a "positive" emotional feeling of admiration or infatuation. It's your admiration of these traits that keeps your treasure buried under the weight of "minimization"; in other words, you imagine yourself to be "less than" someone else so that's what you appear to demonstrate in the world.

— *Keep this in mind:* Every human being has every character trait, as well as its opposite. And all traits can be summarized and concisely written down into a brief phrase of one to four words.

— *Instructions:* Starting in Column 1, "Trait I most like or admire about him or her," use just a few words (no more than four for each trait), to list what you admire and believe to be the most positive. For example, you could write *influential, incredibly creative,* or *handsome.* You'll write only one trait in each space provided in the first column, so allow yourself enough room.

The primary question to ask yourself as you complete Column 1 is: **What human trait, action, or inaction do I most like, admire, or consider positive or attractive about this person?** This trait, action, or inaction could be from any of the seven kinds of treasures you've explored in this book (spiritual, mental, vocational, financial, familial, social, and physical). Also consider temporal categories—the past, present, and future. If you can't think of something that's happening right now, look into the past or project into the future.

Here are some other ways to ask this primary question:

- **What do I most like, respect, or consider positive or attractive about this person?**
- **Why is this person likable?**
- **What has he or she done or not done that felt good?**
- **What makes me seek and admire this person?**
- **Why do I feel good when I think of this person?**
- **Why can't I be away from him or her?**
- **Why do I want to deal with this person or see him or her again?**
- **Why do I desire this person so much?**

Clearly and precisely define the human character trait, action, or inaction you *most* like, admire, or consider positive or attractive about this person. As you write, concentrate on the exact time (when) and space (where, that is, the location in terms of direction and distance) the person expressed this. Write down each trait in one to four words within the space.

— *Confirm that you're done:* Ask yourself, *Are there any more human traits, actions, or inactions that I most like, admire, or consider positive or attractive about this person?*

Column 2

— *Purposes:* To reveal that this perceived "positive" resides in you, too; to reawaken and capture specific memories where people have seen you express this same or similar trait, action, or inaction in one or many forms and to the same degree; to help you realize that people are aware of your expression of this trait and that whatever characteristics you see in others are truly reflected in your own life in some form; to dissolve any infatuation you might have toward the person you're using as a subject; to elevate the minimized or self-depreciative and sacrificed part of yourself back into balance.

— *Keep this in mind:* Human beings have every trait, as well as its opposite. **Don't bother questioning whether you have this quality, because you do. It's not a matter of *if* you possess it, but only *where, when,* and *who* has seen it.**

All characteristics are apparent to someone.

You never gain or lose traits; you only change their form, and your hierarchy of values determines how they're expressed.

Everyone is your reflection: The seer, the seeing, and the seen are the same. In less lofty terms, if you spot it in them, you've got it in you.

— *Instructions:* Go to Column 2, "Initials of people who see this trait in me." In the space next to each positive trait you listed in Column 1, write as many initials as you can, and don't worry about making them legible. As you fill the space, write over the original initials with new ones. The box may become black with ink—it doesn't matter if you can't read it. The point is to acknowledge that others have seen this trait in you. One person may have noticed it many times; others may have seen it once or more. (But don't just write *everybody,* because that's an exaggerated illusion. Be specific.)

As you complete Column 2, ask yourself the following: **Who observes(ed) or recognizes(ed) this human trait in me, in a form/expression either similar to or different from this person's?** It's not a matter of whether you have this, but only a question of *where, when,* and *in what form* it's been noticed by another. For example, if you've written *wonderful dancer,* this doesn't mean that you have to have performed *Swan Lake*. Who perceives you as being graceful, rhythmic, or adept at partnership?

Here are additional ways to ask this primary question:

- **Where and when have I had that character trait, and who's seen it?**
- **Where and when have I exhibited this attribute and others were positively affected by it? Who's witnessed that?**
- **Who's seen me act out this quality? Who else?**

Continue until you can honestly see that you demonstrate this trait to the same degree as the person in question, although it may be in different forms. If you're not completely convinced that you have this characteristic in some regard to an equal extent, then keep writing more initials until you are. This is called truly "owning your golden shadow," and it's one of the essential parts of uncovering your seven secret treasures. Through this process, you reclaim the disowned parts of you that you believe are positive. This could take anywhere from 10 to 50 initials.

Be sure you identify and include who observes or recognizes the trait in you now; otherwise, you might fall into the illusion that you once had the treasure in your possession but you don't anymore.

— *Confirm that you're done:* Ask yourself, *Can I see that I have this human trait, action, or inaction in a similar or different form, and to exactly the same degree, as I observe it in the other person?*

Column 3

— *Purpose:* To further dissolve any remaining infatuation with the person, and to balance any admiration for the character trait itself.

— *Keep this in mind:* Every human trait has two sides, a benefit and a drawback; nothing is one-sided. Everything is neutral until someone judges whether or not it's beneficial, according to his or her hierarchy of values.

When we're infatuated with others, we tend to inject their belief system into our lives and try to change ourselves to be more like them.

— *Instructions:* Move on to Column 3, "How this trait in him or her is a drawback or disservice to me." Write down the abbreviations of the word(s) that represent how the quality, action, or inaction from Column 1 hinders or hindered you (or disserves or disserved you) in all seven areas of life, as well as in the past, present, and future. For example, if you listed *considerate* in Column 1, the Column 3 disadvantages might be that this person's consideration is time-consuming, obligating, and distracting; it fosters expectations, dependency, and infatuation; and it may have a hidden agenda. To save space, these could be abbreviated to something like this: *TC, Obl., Dist., Exp. Dep., Inf., HA*. Shorten your terms in a way that makes sense to you.

The primary question to ask yourself as you complete Column 3 is: **How is the trait I listed in Column 1 a drawback or disservice to me as it's expressed by this person?**

The following are additional ways to ask yourself this:

- **How did or does this character trait act as a disservice to me? How else?**
- **How is what this person did or didn't do a curse to me?**
- **What shortcomings did I observe or receive from the individual expressing this trait?**
- **How or in what way could this attribute impede me?**
- **How could his or her action or inaction impact me negatively?**

Keep writing until you dissolve any admiration or infatuation toward this trait—until you feel neutral about it, and you can see that it has equal benefits and drawbacks. This generally requires at least 15 abbreviated downsides—and often more.

— *Confirm that you're done:* Ask yourself, *Can I see that this trait in him or her has both positive and negative aspects?*

Column 4

— *Purposes:* To dissolve any pride associated with expressing the trait listed in Column 1; to realize that the only way the drawbacks associated with this trait can tarnish your treasures is if you pretend that they don't exist.

— *Keep this in mind:* Elevated pride draws tragedy, challenge, humbling circumstances, and distracting low priorities into our lives.

Everyone displays every trait and its opposite at the same time and to the same degree, such as being generous and stingy, nice and mean, or considerate and inconsiderate.

All qualities have two sides, a benefit and a drawback; no trait is one-sided.

— *Instructions:* Now go to Column 4, "How this trait in me is a drawback or disservice to others." Abbreviate the word(s) representing how your particular expression of the trait listed in Column 1 hinders or hindered others who saw it in you.

The primary question to ask yourself as you complete Column 3 is: **How is the trait I listed in Column 1 a drawback or disservice to others as it's expressed**

by me? Another way to ask this is: **How has acting out my matching characteristic disadvantaged others?**

Keep writing until you dissolve any admiration or infatuation toward this trait in yourself—until you neutralize the pride that you may have had about it. Be mindful of how this can be an obstacle in all seven areas of life. This also generally requires 15 or more abbreviated drawbacks, so write small to allow yourself as much room as possible.

— *Confirm that you're done:* Ask yourself, *Can I see that this trait in me has been both a service and a disservice, a blessing and a curse, to others?*

Column 5

— *Purposes:* To dissolve whatever "all" or "none" and "always" or "never" illusions and labels you may have associated with the person who's the subject of this exercise; to open the doorway to greater communication with that individual.

— *Keep this in mind:* Human beings equally display every trait and its opposite.

— *Instructions:* Go to Column 5, "Initials of those who see in him or her the opposite trait to Column 1." Write the initials of individuals who perceive the person in question as having Column 1's "anti-trait"—the opposite of what you wrote there. Be sure that if the quality listed in Column 1 (for example, *nice*) is directed from the person in question to a particular individual (for example, your brother), then the people you note as seeing the opposite trait *(mean)* know that it's directed toward the same person (your brother), thereby making the method "vector or person specific." In other words, take the time to realize how opposites can be seen within the exact same relationship. This way you can neutralize the lopsided label that you've place on this dynamic. However, if the characteristic is general and not directed toward anyone in particular, then simply identify the people who see the opposite in your subject.

The key question to ask yourself as you complete Column 5 is: **Who observes(ed) or recognizes(ed) the exact opposite trait in him or her, and to the same degree?** (Be vector specific if applicable.)

The following are alternative ways to ask yourself this:

- **Where and when does this person possess the opposite character trait, the anti-trait, and who's seen it?**

- **Where is this person the opposite of what I admire? Who sees him or her this way?**

Keep writing down initials until you can truly sense that there's a perfect balance of the trait and its opposite, or anti-trait, and that there are plenty of people who verify this.

— *Confirm that you're done:* Ask yourself, *Can I see that this person has both sides (trait and anti-trait) equally? Can I acknowledge that he or she acts one way when I support his or her core beliefs and the opposite way when I challenge them? If I learn how to communicate effectively in accordance with this person's higher values, can I now understand that I could experience different outcomes?*

Column 6

— *Purposes:* To expand your awareness of the equal and opposite action, inaction, or characteristic that is simultaneously or synchronously occurring whenever the person in question is expressing the admired trait; to acquaint you with the hidden intelligence and balancing order that's present among all actions and events in the life matrix; to become humbled to the Grand Organized Design.

— *Keep this in mind:* Nothing is ever missing—it simply exists in a form that's not being recognized or acknowledged. All human beings receive a complementary balance of traits from others and within themselves in order to maintain a loving equilibrium; realizing this is "the great discovery."

— *Instructions:* Go to Column 6, "Initials of people who simultaneously did/do the opposite trait to Column 1." Write the initials of whoever was acting out, in the exact same moment, the opposite attribute to the one you listed in Column 1. Again, be vector specific. If the person was nice, considerate, or generous to your brother, for instance, who was observed being mean, inconsiderate, and stingy toward him at the same time? Your answers may include one or many people, male or female, close or distant, real or imagined. If you can recall one side of something, you always have the power to come up with the other angle. Human perception demands such simultaneous contrasts.

Here's an example: Remember my friend who uses this technique to avoid "swelling his head to the size of the moon"? He once told me about a time when he was participating in a documentary as an on-site expert. The people in the studio filming were incredibly complimentary to my friend, telling him that of the 50 other people they'd interviewed, he was the most brilliant person they'd spoken with. The staff admired his wisdom and praised his humility. However, my friend remarked that it was challenging for him not to get sucked into the illusion of his own "superiority." To help bring him back to Earth, he said, the day after he returned from the filming, he received word from a colleague that some individuals had been talking about him while he was gone. These people had complained that he was manipulative, shallow, and "dark." At the exact moment he'd been praised in the studio, he'd been reprimanded behind his back.

As you complete Column 6, ask: **Who is or was acting out the trait opposite to the one in Column 1 at the exact same moment?**

Some other ways to ask this primary question are the following:

- **Who is or was acting out the opposite human trait to the one I like or liked at the exact same moment? Who else?**

- **When this person was positive, accepting, and admiring to me, who was simultaneously negative, rejecting, or critical of me?**

Repeat this step for every instance that you can remember this person acting out this opposite quality, until you can't think of any more times.

— *Confirm that you're done:* Ask yourself, *Can I see that there has been simultaneous expression of this trait and its opposite on every occasion?*

Column 7

— *Purposes:* To dissolve any "nightmares" concerning the person's expression of the trait opposite to the one you've admired; to indirectly dissolve any remaining infatuation with the admired property in Column 1.

— *Keep this in mind:* Everything has two sides, a benefit and a drawback; nothing is one-sided.

Every aspect of life is neutral until someone judges whether or not it's beneficial, according to his or her hierarchy of values.

— *Instructions:* Finish Side A with Column 7, "Benefits that I experience when this person acts out the opposite trait to Column 1." Write down the blessings, the upside, and the benefits to you if the person were to act out the opposite of what you wrote in Column 1.

The paramount question to ask as you complete this column is: **If this person acted out the opposite human trait to the one I wrote in Column 1, what would the benefit be to me?** Another way to ask this question is: **What would the advantage be if this person acted differently than I'd like?**

List abbreviations of the benefits and keep writing until you no longer feel infatuated with the person's expression of the trait in Column 1, and you're not dreading or having nightmares about them being the opposite.

— *Confirm that you're done:* Ask yourself, *Can I clearly see the benefits to me if this person were to demonstrate the opposite trait?*

Instructions for Side B

(*Note:* A copy of the form used for this exercise is included at the end of this Appendix.)

This part of The Demartini Method is designed to balance your *resentments* toward someone by helping you do the following:

- Identify the traits you perceive as negative
- Acknowledge their existence in you
- See how each one can actually serve you and others
- Realize that the opposite traits, which you might have considered "positive," are also present and are being acted out by others
- Recognize what drawbacks might occur if this person were to magically behave in the opposite way

This brings balance, revealing the magnificence in both the world around you and the riches within you.

Column 8

— *Purpose:* To pinpoint the specific, most negatively charged human traits, actions, or inactions that push you away from or repel you from this person—the ones that "hook" you and/or bring out a "negative" emotional feeling of loathing or resentment.

— *Keep this in mind:* Human beings have every trait, as well as its opposite. All characteristics can be summarized and concisely written down into a brief phrase of one to four words.

— *Instructions:* Starting in Column 8, "Trait I dislike or despise most about him or her," use just a few words (no more than four for each one) to list the qualities you despise and believe to be the most negative. For example, you could write *lazy* or *never repays loans* or *lies*. You'll put only one trait in each space provided in this column, so allow yourself enough room.

The primary question to ask as you complete Column 8 is: **What human trait, action, or inaction do I most dislike, despise, or consider negative or repulsive about this person?**

This trait, action, or inaction could be from any of the seven kinds of treasures you've explored in this book: spiritual, mental, vocational, financial, familial, social, and physical. Also consider temporal categories—the past, present, and future. If you can't think of something that's happening right now, look into the past or project into the future.

Here are some other ways to ask this question:

- **What makes him or her unlikable?**
- **What has this person done or not done that feels so bad?**
- **What characteristic does this person demonstrate that angers me?**
- **What can't I like about him or her?**
- **What is it that makes me avoid and despise him or her?**
- **Why do I hurt when I think about this person?**
- **Why can't I be near this individual?**
- **Why don't I want to deal with this person or see him or her again?**
- **What has this person done or not done that I think I haven't or have done?**
- **Why can't I stand him or her?**
- **What negative quality does this person possess that blocks me from loving him or her?**

Clearly and precisely define the human character trait, action, or inaction you *most* dislike. As you write, concentrate on the exact time (when) and space (where, that is, the location in terms of direction and distance) the person expressed this.

— *Confirm that you're done:* Ask yourself, *Are there any more human traits, actions, or inactions that I most dislike, despise, or consider negative or repulsive about this person?*

Column 9

— *Purposes:* To reawaken and capture specific memories where others have seen you express this same or similar trait, action, or inaction in one or many forms and to an equal degree; to help you realize that people are aware of your expression of this trait and that whatever you see in them is truly reflected in your own life in some way; to dissolve any resentment you might have toward the individual whom you're using as a subject; to lower and balance the exaggerated or self-aggrandized and inflated part of yourself.

— *Keep this in mind:* Human beings have every characteristic, as well as its opposite. **Don't bother questioning whether you have this trait, because you do. It's not a matter of *if* you have it, but only *where, when,* and *who* has seen it.** All qualities are apparent to someone.

You never gain or lose anything; you only change the forms. Your hierarchy of values determines how your attributes are expressed.

Everyone is your reflection: The seer, the seeing, and the seen are the same. In less lofty terms, if you spot it in them, you've got it in you.

— *Instructions:* Go to Column 9, "Initials of people who see this trait in me." In the space next to each positive trait you listed earlier, write as many initials as you can and don't worry about making them legible. As you fill the space, write over the original letters with new ones. The box may become black with ink, but it doesn't matter if you can't read it. The point is to acknowledge that others have seen this trait in you. One person may have seen it many times; others may have noticed it once or more. (But don't just write *everybody,* because that's an illusion—be specific. This is a way of integrating your brain and your personas.)

As you complete Column 9, ask yourself the following: **Who observes(ed) or recognizes(ed) this human trait in me, in a form/expression either similar to or different from this person's?** It's not a matter of whether you have this, but only a question of *where, when,* and *in what form* it's been observed by another person. For example, if you've written *stole money from me,* this doesn't mean that you must have literally robbed someone. Who perceives you as having cheated them or taken money or something of value without permission?

Here are some additional ways to ask this primary question:

- **Where and when have I had this characteristic, and who's seen it?**
- **Where and when have I had this character trait that others feel pained by, and who's noticed it?**
- **Who's observed me act this out? Who else?**

Continue until you can honestly see that you demonstrate this trait to the same degree as the person in question, although it may be in different forms. If you're not completely convinced that you have this attribute in some regard and to an equal extent, then keep writing more initials until you are. This is called truly "integrating your shadow." Through this process, you reclaim your disowned parts that you believe are negative. This could take anywhere between 10 and 50 initials.

Be sure that you identify and include those who observe the trait in you *now;* otherwise, you might fall into the illusion that you once had the trait but don't anymore.

— *Confirm that you're done:* Ask yourself, *Can I see that I have this trait, action, or inaction in a similar or different form and to exactly the same degree as I observe it in the other person?*

Column 10

— *Purpose:* To further dissolve any remaining resentment toward the person, and to neutralize any contempt or fear of the characteristic itself.

— *Keep this in mind:* Everything has two sides, a benefit and a drawback; nothing is one-sided.

Every trait is neutral until someone judges whether or not it's beneficial, according to his or her hierarchy of values. When we disapprove of others, we tend to project our belief systems into their lives and try to change them to be more like us.

— *Instructions:* Move on to Column 10, "How this trait in him or her is a benefit or service to me." Think about words that represent how the property in Column 8 helps or helped you (or serves or served you) in all seven areas of life, as well as in the past, present, and future. For example, if you had listed *inconsiderate* in Column 8, the Column 10 benefits might be that this person's lack of consideration frees up your time, doesn't incur obligations, is liberating, creates no expectations, and keeps you from building a fantasy about him or her. To save space, these advantages could be abbreviated something like this: *FT, No Obl., Lib., No Exp., No Fant.*

The primary question to ask yourself as you complete Column 10 is: **How is the human trait I listed in Column 8 a benefit or service to me as it's expressed by this person?**

The following questions are some other ways to ask this:

- **How did this characteristic serve me? How else?**
- **What could be the blessing of what this person did or didn't do?**
- **What advantages did I observe or receive from the individual expressing this trait?**
- **How did this person's action or inaction impact me positively?**

Keep writing until you dissolve any resentment toward or fear of the person and this trait—until you feel neutral and can see that he or she has both benefits and drawbacks. This generally requires at least 15 or more abbreviated benefits.

— *Confirm that you're done:* Ask yourself, *Can I see that his or her trait has equally been a service and a disservice, a blessing and a curse?*

Column 11

— *Purpose:* To dissolve any shame or guilt associated with expressing the trait listed in Column 8.

— *Keep this in mind:* All humans display every trait and its opposite at the same time and to the same degree, such as being generous and stingy, nice and mean, and considerate and inconsiderate. All traits have two sides, a benefit and a drawback; no trait is one-sided.

— *Instructions:* Now go to Column 11, "How this trait in me is a benefit or service to others." Abbreviate the word(s) representing how your particular expression of the trait listed in Column 8 benefits or serves others who see it in you.

The primary question to ask as you complete Column 11 is: **How is the trait I listed in Column 8 a benefit or service to others as it's expressed by me?** Another way to ask this is: **How is my matching characteristic a benefit to those who see me that way?**

Continue writing until you dissolve any resentment or hatred of this quality in yourself. Keep in mind how it can be an advantage in all seven areas of life. This again generally requires at least 15 or more abbreviated benefits, so write small to allow yourself as much room as possible.

— *Confirm that you're done:* Ask yourself, *Can I see that this trait in me has been both a service and a disservice, a blessing and a curse?*

Column 12

— *Purposes:* To dissolve whatever "all" or "none" and "always" or "never" illusions and labels that you may have associated with the person who's the subject of this exercise; to open the doorway to greater communication with that individual.

— *Keep this in mind:* Humans equally display every trait and its opposite.

— *Instructions:* Go to Column 12, "Initials of people who see in him or her the opposite trait to Column 8." Write the initials of individuals who perceive the person in question as having Column 8's "anti-trait" (the opposite of what you wrote there). Be sure that if the quality listed in Column 8 (for example, *mean*) is directed from the person in question to a particular individual (for example, your brother), then the people you note as seeing the opposite trait *(nice)* know that it's directed toward the same person (your brother), thereby making the method vector specific. In other words, take the time to realize how opposites can be seen in the exact same relationship. This way you can neutralize the lopsided label that you've placed on this dynamic. However, if the trait is general, then simply identify the people who see its opposite.

The key question to ask as you complete this column is: **Who observes(ed) or recognizes(ed) the exact opposite human trait in him or her, and to the same degree?** (Be vector specific if applicable.)

Here are more ways to ask this:

- **Where and when does this person possess the opposite characteristic, the anti-trait, and who's seen it?**

- **Where is the individual the opposite of what I resent? Who sees him or her in this way?**

Keep writing initials until you can truly sense that there's a perfect balance of the attribute and its opposite, and that there are plenty of people who verify this.

— *Confirm that you're done:* Ask yourself, *Can I see that this person has both sides (trait and anti-trait) equally? Can I acknowledge that the subject acts one way when I support his or her core beliefs and the opposite way when I challenge them? If I learned how to communicate effectively in accordance with this person's higher values, can I now realize that I could experience different outcomes?*

Column 13

— *Purposes:* To expand your awareness of the equal and opposite action, inaction, or characteristic that simultaneously occurs whenever the person in question expresses the resented trait; to acquaint you with the hidden intelligence and balancing order that's present among all actions and events in the life matrix; to become humbled to the Grand Organized Design.

— *Keep this in mind:* Nothing is ever missing—it simply exists in a form that's not being recognized or acknowledged.

All humans receive a complementary balance of traits from others and within themselves in order to maintain a loving equilibrium—realizing this is "the great discovery."

— *Instructions:* Go to Column 13, "Initials of people who simultaneously did/do the opposite trait to Column 8." Write the initials of whoever was acting out, in that exact same moment, the opposite of what you listed in Column 8. Again, be vector specific. If the person was mean, inconsiderate, or stingy with your brother, for instance, then who was observed being nice, considerate, and generous toward him at the same time? Your answers may include one or many people, male or female, close or distant, real or imagined. If you can recall one side of the story, you always have the power to come up with the other. Human perception demands such simultaneous contrasts.

As you complete Column 13, ask: **Who is or was acting out the human trait opposite to the one in Column 8 at the exact same moment?** (Again, be vector specific if applicable.)

Here are additional ways to ask this primary question:

- **Who is or was acting out the opposite trait to the one I dislike(d) at the exact same moment? Who else?**

- **When this person was negative, rejecting, and critical of me, who was simultaneously positive, accepting, or praising of me?**

Repeat this step for every instance that you can remember this person displaying this opposite attribute until you can't think of anymore.

— *Confirm that you're done:* Ask yourself, *Can I see that there's been simultaneous expression of this trait and its opposite on every occasion?*

Column 14

— *Purposes:* To dissolve any fantasies concerning the person's expression of the trait opposite to the one you've despised; to indirectly dissolve any remaining resentment of the disliked quality in Column 8.

— *Keep this in mind:* Everything has two sides, a benefit and a drawback; nothing is one-sided. Every trait is neutral until someone judges whether or not it's beneficial, according to his or her hierarchy of values.

— *Instructions:* Finish Side B with Column 14, "Drawbacks to me of this person acting out the opposite trait to Column 8." Now you're going to write down the curse, the downside, and the drawbacks to you if the person were to act out the opposite of what you wrote in Column 8.

The foremost question to ask as you complete Column 14 is: **If this person acted out the opposite of what I wrote in Column 8, what would the drawback be to me?** Another way to ask this question is: **What would be the disadvantage if this person were the way I wish him or her to be?**

List the abbreviations of the drawbacks, and keep writing until you no longer feel resentful about the person's expression of the trait in Column 8, and you're not wishing for or having fantasies about him or her being the opposite.

— *Confirm that you're done:* Ask yourself, *Can I clearly see the drawbacks to me if this person were to demonstrate the opposite attribute?*

While Filling Out the Form . . .

Think about all seven secret treasures: mental, physical, spiritual, financial, vocational, familial, and social. **Think chronologically** into the past, present, and future. When the positives outweigh the negatives, you become emotionally attracted and infatuated (addicted). When the positives don't equal the negatives, you lie. Lies are imbalances. When the positives equal the negatives, you become balanced, grateful, and unconditionally loving. The truth is balance!

Please note that you will benefit from listing at least 20 traits in the first column of each side of the form, and then completing the remaining columns accordingly.

The Demartini Method, Side A

Person:

Date:

Column 1	Column 2	Column 3	Column 4	Column 5	Column 6	Column 7
Trait I most like or admire about him or her	Initials of people who see this trait in me	How this trait in him or her is a drawback or disservice to me	How this trait in me is a drawback or disservice to others	Initials of those who see in him or her the opposite trait to Column 1	Initials of people who simultaneously did/do the opposite trait to Column 1	Benefits that I experience when this person acts out the opposite trait to Column 1

(Property of the *Concourse of Wisdom School*)

While Filling Out the Form . . .

Think about all seven secret treasures: mental, physical, spiritual, financial, vocational, familial, and social. **Think chronologically** into the past, present, and future. When the positives outweigh the negatives, you become emotionally attracted and infatuated (addicted). When the positives don't equal the negatives, you lie. Lies are imbalances. When the positives equal the negatives, you become balanced, grateful, and unconditionally loving. The truth is balance!

Please note that you will benefit from listing at least 20 traits in the first column of each side of the form, and then completing the remaining columns accordingly.

The Demartini Method, Side B

Person:

Date:

Column 8	Column 9	Column 10	Column 11	Column 12	Column 13	Column 14
Trait I dislike or despise most about him or her	Initials of people who see this trait in me	How this trait in him or her is a benefit or service to me	How this trait in me is a benefit or service to others	Initials of people who see in him or her the opposite trait to Column 8	Initials of people who simultaneously did/do the opposite trait to Column 8	Drawbacks to me of this person acting out the opposite trait to Column 8

(Property of the *Concourse of Wisdom School*)

→ APPENDIX B ←

Now What? Dealing with "Obstacles"

While completing The Demartini Method, there may be moments when you feel mentally and emotionally challenged. You may long to give up, throw in the towel, or just plain quit; attempting to answer each question sufficiently and completely in all of the columns will probably try your mental faculties at times. These are normal feelings that will wax and wane as you proceed.

There may even be a few moments when you feel that you just can't go another step, let alone complete the method. The difficulty is more often an internal conflict than an actual inability to think out the answers, though. The key is to not let any of these transient emotions stop you from going through with this important and life-changing process. Keep asking yourself how this exercise will help transform your life, which will give you your own incentive to continue. When your "why" is big enough, your "how" will take care of itself.

You may even find yourself, when challenged, coming up with so-called valid reasons as to why you can't continue or come up with the answers. Most all of these excuses are simply that: excuses. Don't let any of them keep you from completing the method. I assure you that the work and effort will be worth it, once you're finished.

In this section, I've listed some common questions and objections that I've heard from thousands of people while helping them through The Demartini Method. Don't let the disempowered you interfere with your stronger self. Refuse to give up and just keep working. If necessary, go on to another column and then come back later to the one that previously stumped you. No matter what, keep digging into your memory and keep working. Let nothing stop you.

Where there's a will, there's a way. Having the incentive or motivation to continue is the key, and the results will be worth whatever challenge you may think that you're facing. So, just keep going until the method is completed. Your heart will thank you, and so will the people you love.

Excuse: I can't think of anything else. Am I done?

Response: When you complete The Demartini Method, you'll notice that you generally:

- Have a poised presence about your countenance

- Feel and observe the presence of the person who was your subject

- Be silent and in deep contemplation over the person you now appreciate and love

- Sense that someone in the room with you resonates with or reminds you of the person who was your subject, and you'll feel a magnetic connection between yourself and him or her

- Shed tears of gratitude and love for the person

- Just "know" when you are truly "done"

When you've completed The Demartini Method forms, ask yourself, *Do I feel deep appreciation and love for this person?*

If your answer is no, then identify what's still in the way of you appreciating and loving the person you've chosen as your subject. Specify what the emotionally charged trait is that still pushes your buttons, return to the worksheet, and complete however many more lines needed to be truly appreciative and loving.

If your answer is yes, then in your mind's eye, imagine that the person is sitting in front of you. Ask yourself, *What is in my heart that I'd love to share with this special person, who's now sitting before me in my mind's eye?* Imagine if this were your last chance to speak to this person; what would you love to say to him or her from your heart?

Even if the individual didn't change a thing, could you open your heart and love the person just as he or she is?

Is there anything still in the way of appreciating and loving this person? What does your heart say? When was the last time you hugged this person? Would you like to do so right now?

You'll experience the following signs of wisdom and illumination if you've truly completed The Demartini Method:

- Tears of inspiration
- Unconditional gratitude
- Unconditional love
- Certainty of truth
- Nonlocal "presence" of loved one
- Fearlessness and guiltlessness
- Speechlessness—outward silence
- Reduced inner mind noise
- Balance, centeredness, and integration
- Eased tensions and compressions
- Lightness and weightlessness
- Desire to embrace
- Uplifting of head and eyes
- Truly elevated self-worth
- "Domino effect"—a fuller understanding of past events

Excuse: I don't know if I can I do this by myself without anyone's help.

Response: Yes, you can. Thousands of people have succeeded in completing this method beautifully without any outside help. There's certainly no harm in receiving aid, but if the instructions are followed completely, the method takes care of itself while you're working alone.

Excuse: I don't know (or I can't think of) any more answers for a particular column.

Response: Yes, you do know and can think of more, so keep digging into your memories for the answers! It's not uncommon for people to run into momentary mental (memory) blocks while they actively work on this. Don't be alarmed or discouraged; simply continue to concentrate on the question at hand and know with certainty that you have the answer within your mind. (This has been proven by tens of thousands of cases.) Keep going and looking within; giving up isn't an option.

Excuse: I haven't known this person long enough to be able to complete the process.

Response: If you've known the subject long enough to be upset or infatuated with him or her, then you know enough to identify the opposites. Keep working.

When we interact with a person and create our perceptions, we filter out much of what we take in from our conscious mind. We selectively allow in and delete out perceptions that support or challenge our personal values. When we feel that it supports our values, the positive information is allowed into our conscious memories and the negative is stored in our unconscious. In turn, when we feel that it challenges our values, negative data is allowed to surface, and the positive is kept hidden.

All the information is there, yet our values selectively filter what we consciously remember. Sometimes it takes diligent probing to dig out the other, emotionally charged half of the information from our unconscious memories. So it's not that you can't remember, because you can. It's just that you must probe beneath your selective filter. If you interacted with and experienced the person at all, then both positively and negatively charged information is available. All events are neutral and balanced until our conscious values filter gets a hold of them. Keep looking; giving up isn't an option.

Excuse: There's no way you can say that I have the same trait to the same degree as this person.

Response: After examining more than 4,600 human character traits in one of the largest dictionaries available, I discovered that everyone displays (in some form or another) every known positive and negative quality. Each person's hierarchy of values determines how these attributes appear, but you'll find that they're all there if you inspect closely. We require them to survive in the world, so it's not a matter of *if* you have them; it's a matter of *in what form* you display them. Whatever you see in others you have within yourself.

Keep digging. People often don't want to admit to themselves that they display certain shadowy character traits. Yet no matter how hard you try to rid yourself of certain characteristics, they don't disappear. They simply become repressed or hidden from your conscious memories for a while until they're forced into your awareness.

Our pride often blocks us from seeing our true natures, but it's possible, so keep looking.

Excuse: I don't think I can find drawbacks to some character trait that I believe is good or benefits in something that I believe is bad.

Response: Each quality is actually neutral (neither good nor bad) until some person with a set of projected values labels it; good and bad are merely perceptions. It's up to you to see beyond your own filter and projections in order to get to the truth of the characteristic and discover this inherent balance. In other words, one person's food is another's poison.

By remaining fixated in your initial moral or ethical view, you allow the trait in question to run your life; but by neutralizing your perception, you set yourself free. Keep looking for the drawbacks. Giving up isn't an option.

Excuse: I don't have a problem with anyone.

Response: If you don't have such a challenge, you'd be wise to get on your knees and pray for one. Without something to work on, we die or give up on life. If you're on this earth and have a body, I'm certain you can find someone or something you feel strongly about, so look again.

Excuse: I can't think of anyone I hate.

Response: Maybe *hate* isn't the word to use. Think of someone whom you strongly dislike or who aggravates or frustrates you.

Excuse: I don't want to think of the person that way.

Response: Is that because you want to hold on to your current perception of that individual? The truth sets you free, while your illusions imprison you. Ecstatic fantasies are accompanied by torturing nightmares. When you realize that you're complete in and of yourself, you'll have no reason to fear writing down those traits, for each one will be balanced by its opposite and appreciated and loved.

Excuse: My therapist said it was better for me to hate this person.

Response: I'm not necessarily telling you to disobey your therapist. But he or she may not be familiar with The Demartini Method and, therefore, may not know how it can help you dissolve your anger and get on with your life. Carrying around such feelings has been shown to disturb your health and other areas of your life. If, after you finish, you'd prefer to go back to being upset, you certainly may.

Excuse: I've already worked out all my problems with the person.

Response: If you still describe them as past *problems,* then there's likely to still be some charge associated with them. Would you like to have them not run your life anymore? Then let's keep working.

Excuse: I haven't done as much as that person has.

Response: What you see in others is a reflection of you. Who has seen you do that? Who else? Don't let yourself lie to yourself. Look again—sometimes you've done the same thing in a different form.

Excuse: I've never done that.

Response: If you discover that you're stuck on a particular event that you believe you haven't done in the physical sense (such as *I've never killed anyone*), look into all seven areas of your life and find the ways you've "killed" others with your thoughts, words, or actions. Remind yourself that there are many ways to "kill" someone and that everyone has every trait in some form.

Excuse: You don't understand that this person really hurt me.

Response: I understand that you currently feel that this person hurt you. Now, would you like to have that emotion continue to run your life, or would you love to be set free? If you complete this process, you'll no longer perceive him or her as having injured you. Instead, you'll realize that this individual also provided you with an equal opportunity for pleasure. If you'll just continue working the process, you'll set yourself free and discover how this damage can be dissolved and you can become re-empowered. Every minute you spend thinking about your pain reduces a minute that you can feel set free.

Realize, too, that your perceptions caused you to suffer more than their actions did.

Excuse: There's no way I'll be able to "balance" them.

Response: That's what many people say when they begin. But so far everyone has been able to do so completely in the end. I'm certain that you will, too—so keep working. Instead of thinking about how you can't, just get working on balancing them.

Excuse: This person is evil. There's no way I'll be able to find any good in him or her.

Response: Everyone has two sides, and all events have both benefits and drawbacks. What you see in others is simply a reflection of yourself. If you don't want this person to continue to run your life, then keep working.

Excuse: I already forgave this person for the terrible things he or she did to me.

Response: If you still imagine someone as having done something terrible to you, then you still have an emotional charge toward him or her and are letting yourself be controlled by another. You can still liberate yourself further, for the truth of love sets you free. Anything you fear or condemn will continue to run your life until you embrace it. So keep looking for the benefits until you have nothing to forgive and only feel love and appreciation.

Excuse: But I don't want to love and appreciate this person.

Response: It has been my experience that the very people we feel this way about are the ones who are reminding us of the parts of ourselves that we haven't yet learned how to appreciate. Those you say that you don't want to care for are actually the ones that you *do* want to be able to cherish from within. This is because others are our reflections. Deep inside our hearts, love is patiently waiting to surface. You have nothing to lose by feeling affection for them. When you can do so, you can also embrace the part of you that they represent.

Excuse: I'm not close friends with this person anymore.

Response: That's fine. If you choose not to be close to this person, that's your decision. From taking tens of thousands of people through this amazing method, it's been my experience that they're able to love and appreciate others so much more than if they carried the burden of having to avoid or reject them. The process gives you the freedom to have people in or out of your life with greater equanimity. They deserve to be loved for who they are, just as you do, and this method enables you to do exactly that.

Excuse: I think I picked the wrong person to fill out The Demartini Method on, so I doubt I'll get anything out of it.

Response: You can do The Demartini Method on anyone and still benefit, but it's wisest to complete it for someone who still pushes your buttons the most.

Excuse: I'd like to start on someone else.

Response: Don't begin again until you've finished the process for this individual. It's wiser to complete one than to half complete two. Don't move on unless you truly feel that you perceive the other person as more of a button pusher.

Excuse: I didn't get enough sleep last night, so I'm tired and sleepy.

Response: Stop writing for a moment, stand up, and go for a brief walk to get your entire body moving. Have a light snack and some water if you're also hungry. Then sit back down and close your eyes. Think about what you're truly grateful for in life (which will help open your heart, clear your mind, and revitalize you) and meditate for 15 minutes, remaining in a sitting position while taking deep, full breaths. When you're done, then get back to completing the method.

Excuse: I'm worn out and can't go on.

Response: This will pass. Just keep working, unless, of course, you had no sleep last night. If so, why don't you meditate for 15 minutes? This will help you feel refreshed. Then get back to work—I promise that it will be worth it.

Excuse: I'm hungry.

Response: If you're truly hungry, go get a small protein snack, and then come back, get to work, and complete the method. But be sure that this isn't an avoidance mechanism on your part. If it is, just get to work.

Excuse: I don't feel well.

Response: If you feel woozy and need to vomit, feel free to do so . . . and then come back and get to work. Many people have felt dizzy or slightly ill until they finished, and then they were fine. Just keep going.

Excuse: I have a headache.

Response: Ask someone close to you to massage your scalp, have a chiropractic adjustment, take a natural aspirin, or meditate for 15 minutes and then get back to completing the method. Generally, headaches will subside and pass if you just keep working toward your goal.

Excuse: I can't think—or don't want to think—of anything else.

Response: Yes, you can. I hear this excuse weekly, but everyone completes the method. The results are worth the effort. The ideas will come in spurts, so keep working. You can do it! (By the way, the brain doesn't stop thinking.) I know you can complete this.

Excuse: I'm mentally shut down and my brain is fried.

Response: Stop for just a moment, go for a brief walk, move and stretch your head and neck, write down ten ways in which completing this method will help transform your life and enable you to fulfill your highest values, and then get back to completing the method. You'll tend to shut down whenever you can't see how this will help you meet your most important goals. In order to say that you're brain-dead, your brain actually has to be alive. Keep working—I assure you that this is worth completing.

Excuse: I'm not sure that the effects I've experienced will last.

Response: Whatever character trait you've truly balanced through this process will no longer be the button or emotionally charged quality that runs your life. If you leave the method incomplete, that same characteristic will keep troubling you until it's truly brought to balance and completely collapsed. You aren't designed to stop growing mentally and emotionally, so expecting yourself to have no more strong reactions is unrealistic. But a goal to no longer be set off by any one specific trait is reasonable. Complete the method and watch the results.

ABOUT THE AUTHOR

Dr. John F. Demartini is an international speaker and consultant who breathes life and enthusiasm into his audiences with his enlightening perspectives, humorous observations of human nature, and practical action steps. When he speaks, hearts open, minds become inspired, and people are motivated into action. His gentle, fun, and informative teachings mingle entertaining stories with transformational wisdom and insights. His trailblazing philosophy and revolutionary understanding are reshaping modern psychology and business and transforming the lives of millions. As a retired chiropractor, researcher, writer, and philosopher, his studies have made him a leading expert on healing, human potential, and philosophy.

Dr. Demartini is the founder of the Demartini Human Research and Education Foundation, which includes the Studies of Wisdom research and the Concourse of Wisdom educational divisions. He is also the creator of The Breakthrough Experience® seminar and originator of The Demartini Method® and The Great Discovery™. He has written several dozens of books, including the bestsellers *Count Your Blessings: The Healing Power of Gratitude and*

Love; The Breakthrough Experience: A Revolutionary New Approach to Personal Transformation; How to Make One Hell of a Profit and Still Get to Heaven; You Can Have an Amazing Life . . . in Just 60 Days; and *The Heart of Love: How to Go Beyond Fantasy to Find True Relationship Fulfillment.*

Articles and feature stories about Dr. Demartini and his insightful personal and professional development methodologies have appeared in numerous international magazines and newspapers. He's appeared on hundreds of radio and television news and talk shows and several film documentaries. As a presenter, Dr. Demartini has shared his transformative principles and methodologies in conferences with business executives, health professionals, financial managers, and consultants working in the field of human consciousness; and he has presented alongside many of the most well-respected speaking professionals today. As a pioneer on the frontier of human consciousness and an explorer of the ultimate nature of reality, Dr. Demartini is also a leader in the field of psycho-spiritual development and transformation.

In addition, Dr. Demartini is a private consultant, advising people from all walks of life on personal and professional development and achievement. These include Wall Street financiers, corporate executives, health professionals, politicians, Hollywood stars, and sports personalities. His many clients use his expertise and wisdom to assist in keeping their lives, health, relationships, attitudes, and business acumen steadily on track.

For more information:
(888) DEMARTINI or (713) 850-1234
Fax: 713-850-9239
www.DrDemartini.com

NOTES

NOTES

NOTES

NOTES

NOTES

NOTES

NOTES

NOTES

NOTES

Hay House Titles of Related Interest

YOU CAN HEAL YOUR LIFE, the movie,
starring Louise L. Hay & Friends
(available as a 1-DVD program and an expanded 2-DVD set)
Watch the trailer at: **www.LouiseHayMovie.com**

BEING IN BALANCE: *9 Principles for Creating Habits to Match Your Desires,* by Dr. Wayne W. Dyer

COURAGEOUS DREAMING: *How Shamans Dream the World into Being,* by Alberto Villoldo, Ph.D.

THE INTUITIVE SPARK: *Bringing Intuition Home to Your Child, Your Family, and You,* by Sonia Choquette

KICK UP YOUR HEELS . . . BEFORE YOU'RE TOO SHORT TO WEAR THEM: *How to Live a Long, Healthy, Juicy Life,* by Loretta LaRoche

THE LAW OF ATTRACTION: *The Basics of the Teachings of Abraham®,* by Esther and Jerry Hicks

THE POWER IS WITHIN YOU, by Louise L. Hay

THE POWER OF INTENTION: *Learning to Co-create Your World Your Way,* Dr. Wayne W. Dyer

THE RECONNECTION: *Heal Others, Heal Yourself,* by Dr. Eric Pearl

YOUR SOUL'S COMPASS: *What Is Spiritual Guidance?* by Joan Borysenko, Ph.D., and Gordon Franklin Dveirin, Ed.D.

All of the above are available at your local bookstore, or may be ordered by contacting Hay House (see next page).

HAY
HOUSE